In a time long ago, in a place perhaps like one in your family's lore . . .

Mable and her older sister, Frances—both carrot-topped, and both in dire need of having their tonsils removed—were on the way to the country hospital. All through the trip, in the wagon, the two youngsters debated which of them would go first for the dreaded procedure.

"You're the youngest. You do it," urged Frances, four-and-a-half years Mable's senior.

"No, you're older than me. You do it," begged Mable.

In those days, just after the turn of the last century, tonsils were yanked out without benefit of anesthesia. A mere injection to the throat was all the doctor would use to kill the pain.

Mable sat anxiously by Papa in the waiting room while the doctor began working on Frances behind closed doors. No whimper of protest emerged.

"Maybe this isn't so bad after all," Mable thought, a little relieved. She began to remember the cool, soothing Lemon Ice-Box Pie that Mama and her oldest sister, Bonnie, were making at home while they waited for the girls' return.

After a bit, Frances staggered through the door. Mable saw that her sister's cheeks were puffed out with gauze. *She's alive. Frances survived this. I can, too,* Mable kept reminding herself as she made her way to the doctor's chair and braced for the procedure. She tried not to glance over at the syringe with its needle long as an ice-pick and all the other mysterious instruments that made her flesh creep as Doc Janes prepared to use them.

But within seconds, her screams began. Blood-curdling, terrorizing screams that practically could be heard back at their Brushy Mound home. Papa and Frances listened in horror. What had gone wrong with Mable? Hadn't the pain-killer worked? What about Bonnie, who was a prospective candidate for a tonsillectomy? How would they ever drag her down to Doc Janes' hospital if Mable went home and told about screaming bloody murder?

Recipes, rollicking tales from the farm with the Three Red-Haired Miller Girls . . .

But as for you, continue in what you have learned and have become convinced of, because you know those from whom you learned it.

2 Timothy 3:14

Way Back in the Country

in the

*Recipes from six generations
of East Texas farm cooking
and the stories behind them*

Kay Wheeler Moore

Hannibal Books
P.O. Box 461592
Garland, TX 75046

4

ISBN 0-929292-50-2

Library of Congress Control Number: LC 2002102744

(Use coupons in back to order extra copies of this
and other books
from HANNIBAL BOOKS)

Unless otherwise noted, all Scripture quotations are taken from the
Holy Bible, *New International Version*, copyright 1973, 1978, 1984 by
International Bible Society.

Scripture portions marked KJV are from the *King James Version.*

Hannibal Books
P.O. Box 461592
Garland, Texas 75046-1592

1-800-747-0738
1-972-487-7960 (FAX)
hannibalbooks@earthlink.net
www.hannibalbooks.com

To the memory of
Bonnie (1905-1983)

To *Frances*

and

To my mother,
Little Red

Thank you for

the stories,

the food,

and especially,
the faith

Contents

Foreword

*

Having grown up in East Texas (in Mineola in Wood County), the *Way Back in the Country* cookbook evokes the food of my childhood. I can instantly recall sitting on the back steps consuming big, lush tomatoes as if they were candy, perching on layers of newspaper on top of the ice-cream maker while everyone took turns cranking fresh peach ice cream and helping snap crowder, lady cream peas, or black-eyed peas.

The food of the East Texas I knew is decidedly Southern—fried chicken with cream gravy, corn-on-the-cob, fried okra and other summer vegetables, biscuits, corn bread, hot rolls, homemade sausage, and bread-and-butter pickles. I was Food Editor of the *Houston Chronicle* for almost 35 years, and many of these treasured recipes worked their way into the Food Section even as Houston developed an appreciation for more worldly cuisine.

Thanks to Kay Moore for taking us back to simpler times and introducing us to those who share a common heritage around the dining table.

Ann Criswell
Food Editor, *Houston Chronicle*
1966-2000

Preface

*

If your family is anything like mine, a time-honored recipe is often more than a simple "how-to" of directions for making a food dish.

Behind each list of ingredients for a favorite pie or casserole usually lie stories of life and love that intertwine with your family history through many generations.

The mere aroma of a certain batch of cookies baking may send you on a memory trip to special, bygone places that are dear to your heart and to thoughts of people that have long ago left this earth.

Often your family's triumphs and heartaches, adventures and victories can be traced through its cooking—its comfort food, its celebrations, its holiday treats.

My family, the Miller-Harris clan depicted in this book, has its roots in rural East Texas in a county called Delta, so named because of its triangular shape like the fourth letter of the Greek alphabet. Our six generations of tales begin in the days just after the turn of the last century, proceed on through the Great Depression years, continue through post-World War II, and see Baby Boomers become parents with Computer-Age offspring.

Your own kin may hail from an entirely different era or part of the world, with characters and figures unlike any described in these pages. But as you read the Three Red-Haired Miller Girls' stories and try their recipes and those of their ancestors and progeny, I hope you will be inspired to jot down and preserve a little of your own family lore, if you haven't done this already. That way your children and future generations can experience not only the cooking directions you pass on but will know the people and traditions behind them, even after you are no longer around to spin the yarns in person.

In the meantime, happy reading and happy cooking.

Kay Wheeler Moore
October, 2002
Garland, Texas

ONE

Enter, Little Red

*

The November dawn broke early as the man trudged across the muddy field to the nearby farm house. The amber rim of sun edging onto the horizon was the same shade as his tousled hair, which hadn't seen a comb in a good while now. He mopped his brow, stuffed his kerchief back into the deep front pocket of his coveralls, and readied his arms to embrace his two oldest daughters, were they to be awake at this hour.

"Still sawin' logs in there, but bet they'll pop up f'sure, minute they see ya," announced the apron-clad woman who greeted him at the door. Her boots still wore the black, Delta County mud from her own recent trek across the pasture. Grandma Harris believed it was her ironclad duty to preside over as many of her grandchildren's births as possible. This most recent one, number 30 in the next generation of Harrises, had kept her up all night. She looked as weary as did her son-in-law.

Shivering from the kitchen's early-morning chill, the man passed through to the corner of the parlor, where he knelt by the pallet that Grandpa had assembled on the floor, as best he could, to sleep the girls. Two carrot-colored manes roused in an instant.

"Papa! Papa!" they squealed almost in unison as they bolted from sleep. "Can we go home with you?" cried Bonnie, the older of the two, at 6. "We wanna see our mama," her sister Frances, one year her junior, pleaded.

The two little moppets had been sent over to Grandma and Grandpa Harris' yesterday, about the time old Doc Janes had arrived at their place in the country. Trips across the pasture to their grandparents' house were usually a highlight for the sisters, but yesterday's had been different, somehow. A lot of whispering and scurrying surrounded this departure. Mama had been taken to bed, moaning and clutching her belly. Grandma had disappeared almost as soon as they arrived, leaving them in Grandpa's care.

None of that mattered now, because Papa had come for them. "Yup, let's bundle ya up and get ya back t' the house. Gotta surprise for ya t' see," he smiled. He threw one of Grandma's colorful quilts over each of the gown-clad sisters.

"A surprise? Is it candy?" Frances chirped. Papa always brought stick candy home for the girls after his trips to town.

"Did you bring peanut butter stick? It's my favorite," Bonnie asked. If he had, Bonnie hoped there was one stick for each of them. She knew that she, as the oldest, would probably have to dutifully settle for horehound and turn the peanut butter one over to Frances if Papa had brought only one stick of her special flavor.

"Better 'n candy," their father replied, as he hoisted them both to his shoulders. Then Frances remembered the phone call, heard in a haze, when Grandpa had answered the persistent ring that came in the wee hours of the morning.

"Got 'nother l'il red-haired girl down thar," Grandpa had called out to the girls, who stirred briefly on their mats when their sleep was broken by the phone blare.

"I know!" Frances exclaimed to her father. "It's a baby sister. That's what you have to show us."

Bonnie also remembered what Grandpa had said. "Can we see our sister? Can we go right now?" Bonnie begged.

"I'll see what we can do," Papa answered them. "Come 'long, now. Say 'bye t' Grandma. She'll probably be over later."

As he passed back through the kitchen, comfortably warming now as the pot-bellied stove fired up for breakfast, he sat his two bundles down on the porch momentarily and turned back to nod to Grandma in departure.

"Family's grown a-gin," Grandma mused, stirring up some biscuits as she looked her daughter's husband thoughtfully. "Mattie say what name she's got picked out for th' new young'un?"

"Waaal, I think she'd like to name her Mabel, for her l'il auntie," he answered. Mabel was the youngest of the fourteen children born to Grandma. At age 15 and the only one still at home, Mabel Harris was more like an older sister to Papa's girls than she was an aunt. "An' she promised Doc Janes she'd also call 'er Evelyn, for his wife, since he's delivered all 'er babies."

Grandma nodded her approval as she spooned the biscuits onto her pan.

"Then ole Doc, he sez, 'Miss Mattie, it don' make much diff'ernce what ya name 'er,'" Papa went on. "Everwhar she goes, she'll have just one nickname—L'il Red. The Three Red-Haired Miller Girls. That's what you got now, Mr. Mark,' Doc tells me."

In years to come, Delta County, Texas, would go on to be celebrated for the cotton that grew from its fertile, black soil. A large, pretty state park with a recreational lake would spring up on its borders. Two professional football players who hailed from Cooper, Delta's county seat, would certainly put their hometown in Texas' fifth-smallest county on the map.

But the Three Red-Haired Miller Girls, whose group moniker was coined that very morning, November 26, 1911, as Little Red made her arrival, would make an indelible imprint, as well. In the pages ahead, I'll tell you more about

14

them and about the delicious cooking that was always inter-
twined with their lives, even as far back as the fluffy biscuits
like Grandma Harris made.

Country Biscuits

4 cups all-purpose flour
3 teaspoons baking powder
1 teaspoon salt
1 teaspoon sugar
3/4 cup solid all-vegetable shortening
1 3/4 cups milk

In mixing bowl, sift flour and dry ingredients. Add shortening and milk and work
with hands on lightly floured board. Roll out
and cut with biscuit cutter. Bake at 400 to 425
degrees. Bake until brown (usually 10 to 12
minutes). Makes 20 large biscuits.

T W O

The Cotton Gin Scare

*

These early tales, of course, are not ones I witnessed personally. "Little Red", or Mable Evelyn Miller Wheeler, entered the world on that November Sunday almost four decades before I did, on a much later day in November. (Named "Mabel" for her aunt, she later changed the spelling of her first name because she thought it should look like "table.")

But because she, as my mother, loved to spin family yarns, and because she and her two flame-tressed sisters loved to spend the Sunday afternoons of our family gatherings driving over the deserted roads which once formed the country lanes of their childhoods, all those stories came alive for me time and again. As the Three Red-Haired Miller Girls verbally recreated their growing-up days, I could almost hear the conversations of yesteryear and smell the aroma of the feasts surrounding their fun times.

Here's more of their best:

"Let's push her around in the wheelbarrow."

"No, let's play dress up. She can be the baby."

Bonnie and Frances whispered and giggled as they crept into the bedroom the three sisters shared. Mable, now age 6, was the object of their search. Bonnie and Frances wanted to have some fun on a Saturday afternoon. The plotted all the things that an 11- and 10-year-old could do to a younger sibling once they located her.

Mable wasn't turning up so readily.

"Mama, Mama," called Bonnie after a few more minutes of futile effort. "Seen Mable anywhere?"

Mattie looked up from her kitchen table where she was cutting out a dress to sew for a neighbor.

"Naw, chile, not in a while," their mother answered. "I 'spect she's somewhere with 'er tablet." Mable loved to practice her newly acquired pen strokes that she was learning in first grade.

But another thorough scour of the place proved futile for the two sisters. Bonnie and Frances put aside their prankish plans. They took on faces that were grave and ashen.

"Mama!" Frances wailed, a little quiver in her voice now. "She's not ANYwhere. We can't find her. Honest, Mama."

Mattie's face soon mirrored the concern of her daughters. "Lawsy, chile. You don' s'pose she's gone and got into the cotton gin." The gin was the big machine that separated the seeds, hulls, and other foreign material from the actual cotton. It was close enough to the Miller house for even a six-year-old to gain access.

"Oh, no," Bonnie shrieked, as that prospect sank in. "Let's go get Papa. We gotta find her." Bonnie tugged at her mother's arm. Mother and her oldest were out the door in a flash, aimed toward the gin.

Papa was on the horizon, headed in from the field with one of the mules. Dust flew as Mattie and her daughter sped toward him, in hopes of expanding the search party.

Suddenly, Frances' squeals could be heard for miles.

"She's he-e-e-re. I found her." By Frances' side was a drowsy Mable, rubbing her eyes from sleep and wondering what the fuss was about.

Moments later, after hugs all around and a few relieved tears of rejoicing, the story was pieced together: Mable had fallen asleep on a trunk by a fireplace that jutted out and practically obscured the trunk. As she had made one last comb-through around the house, Frances spotted her sister in the unintentional hiding place. Mable was oblivious to every-one's worry but was, thankfully, safe.

The Miller house was full of joy that evening, with grati-tude that Mable hadn't fallen into the cotton gin after all. And because the Three Red-Haired Miller Girls loved them more than anything, Mattie just well might have treated them to their favorite Orange Balls, so glad was she that her family was all safe and sound and together again.

Orange Balls

1 (12-ounce) package vanilla wafers
1 (1-pound) box powdered sugar
1/2 cup (1 stick) margarine, melted
1 (6-ounce) can frozen orange juice
    concentrate, melted
1 cup pecans, finely chopped
1 (3 1/2-ounce) can flaked coconut

Crush vanilla wafers. Mix in powdered
sugar, melted margarine, melted orange juice
concentrate, and pecans. Shape mixture into
small balls and roll in chopped pecans. Store
in refrigerator or freezer to allow balls to
solidify. Then roll balls in 1 can coconut.
Makes 5 dozen balls.

THREE

The Tale of Little Button

*

Few people but Mable thought Button was very smart—that is, until the day the big storm came.

Button was a small horse. That's where he got his name. He belonged to the Miller family, as part of the team that Papa used to plow. But to tell the truth, he did more service as a horse for Bonnie, Frances, and Mable to hitch up and ride than he did duty as a work animal.

He was so gentle and sweet-natured that anybody could handle him—anyone that treated him respectfully, that is. But one day, Ralph Harris, a cousin of the Three Red-Haired Miller Girls, saw Mable out on Button. He couldn't resist putting Button to the test. Mable, who had grown to be all of eight years old by then, was riding Button around in the yard, just minding her own business.

About that time, Ralph, a lanky fellow with legs as long as stilts, ran up from behind and jumped on Button, behind Mable, yelling "Yippie-ti-yi" like he thought he was a rodeo cowboy.

Poor, scared Button couldn't help himself. He began bucking like a bronco. He threw Mable sailing into the air. She barely missed scraping the barbed-wire fence with her forehead before she landed on the ground with an earth-shattering thud.

Ralph hadn't expected such a calamity. He had only meant to have a little fun. He scooped Mable up and, quick as lighting, slid into the house, unfurling Mable onto the bed. Mattie and Mable's two sisters trailed him in a panic.

"Oh, Aunt Mattie. Call the doctor. Do something. Oh, poor little Mable. I think I killed her." His moans were so loud and piteous that they brought Mable to right then and there. She opened her eyes and blinked at the terrified ones gathered around her. There was nothing wrong with her at all except having the breath soundly knocked out of her.

"Oh, Mable. I didn't mean it," Ralph continued as his russet-haired cousin revived.

"It's that blamed Button," Mattie clucked. "He don' have much sense."

Mable knew differently. And the little horse prove it when the big storm happened.

On that day, the air had been clammy and still. Mattie had looked out the window more than once, her brows knitting with concern.

"Sure be glad t' see yer Papa head on in," she said to Bonnie, who was stirring up some corn bread in the kitchen.

Early that morning, Papa had taken the mule team out to plow. The mules were the Millers' livelihood, as teams were to most rural families in Delta County in those days. It was time to ready the fields for cotton planting. Papa and the team needed every hour of daylight they could muster to get their important work done.

The clouds were thickening into a dark, churning brew.

"Where can yer Papa be?" Mama worried further. She was pacing now, her anxious steps keeping time with the claps of thunder that inched closer by the second.

Just as the rain began pouring in sheets, the metal door of the barn slammed loudly. A drenched Papa appeared at the back porch.

"It come up in a hurry," Papa said of the storm, as he shed muddy boots and cast a worried glance behind him. "No time t' unharness th' team."

Just at that moment, lightning struck close.

"Yow!" yelled Bonnie. She almost dropped the pan of corn bread she was pulling from the oven. "It shocked me!"

"Lookee! Lookee!" screamed Frances. She peered out the window, facing the barn, just as lightening hit. "It's a fireball down there." Everyone ran to the window at once.

Then Button, the little pony with no sense, some thought, stepped up to the door of the barn and began pawing it.

"Something's wrong out there!" cried Mable. "Button knows it, too."

The next few minutes seemed to drag by in slow motion until the storm passed over, the rain slowed to a drizzle, and Papa could get to the barn.

A horrifying scene awaited him. The mules, left in their harnesses, all lay dead on the barn floor. The metal bits on the harnesses had conducted electricity when lightning struck the barn. It got them instantly.

"Oh, no! How will yer Papa ever plow without th' team?" Mattie mourned, in tears. All the girls cried, too.

Through her tears, Mable couldn't help but be a little proud of the pony, Button, who sounded the warning cry as though he sniffed out disaster and alerted the family.

Everyone's tears turned to smiles not many days later when the Miller family's thoughtful neighbors took up a donation and brought them a new team.

It was a good while before the Millers could dine on corn bread without thinking of the strike to the barn that brought catastrophe to the family. But corn bread, to Mable, would also call up another memory—a good one—a memory of the day that little Button proved that big things come in small packages.

Golden Corn Bread

1 cup corn meal
1 cup all-purpose flour
1/4 cup sugar (optional)
4 teaspoons baking powder
1/2 teaspoon salt
1 egg
1 cup milk
1/4 cup solid all-vegetable shortening, soft-
    ened

Sift together corn meal, flour, sugar, baking
powder, and salt into bowl. Add egg, milk,
and shortening. Beat with rotary beater until
smooth, about 1 minute. Bake in greased 8-
inch square pan at 425 degrees for 20 to 25
minutes. Serves 8.

F O U R

Screaming Bloody Murder

*

In some circles, three can be a crowd. With the Red-Haired Miller Girls, three was more often trouble.

The time that the Indian arrived to pick up his dress was a case in point.

The dress was one for his wife that the Indian man (we would more correctly call him a "Native American" today) asked the Miller Girls' mother, Mattie, to sew for him.

The girls couldn't recall ever seeing an Indian squaw visit the house to determine if the garment fit her properly. But Mattie's sewing was like that. She could look at a set of measurements, take an existing pattern, and nip in a little here and expand a little there. The resulting dress went on like a glove. Never mind that Mattie had never laid eyes on the customer. The creation in fabric would be perfect, like a second skin on the lucky wearer.

Extraordinarily gifted, Mattie could spot a garment pictured in a magazine ad, walk to her cutting table, sketch out a pattern, and sew an exact replica. She could admire a dress on the racks at the priciest clothing store, step outside, and scribble out or draw enough details to faithfully copy the same thing on her own sewing machine.

Her girls, of course, wore the fanciest dresses around and were the envy of all. No such thing in their closets as a simple, basic, school dress. Even the clothes they wore to the fields to pick cotton might have ruffles and tucks and top-stitching and elaborate appliques. The Millers were anything but people of means, but the Red Haired-Miller Girls thought themselves to be princesses. No one could compete with their exquisite attire—all from Mattie's hands.

Everyone wanted a garment stitched by the talented Miss Mattie. So when a Native American man who hired on as a day laborer to help with the farming tasks around those parts heard that she took in sewing from the public, he got in line with his order, too.

The Miller Girls spotted him walking down the road, headed there to pick up the dress. They were hanging out the second-story window of their house, where they had a birds'-eye view of the world, or so it felt.

Bonnie, Frances, and Mable crouched under the window sill and giggled as this unusual visitor, a leathery-skinned man with high cheekbones and a braid of black hair hanging halfway down his back, knocked at the door.

"My dress. How much?" he asked in broken sentences. The girls snickered again and peered a tiny bit over the ledge to eyeball the transaction. Mattie returned with the garment, wrapped in brown paper and tied with white string. Payment was exchanged, and the man turned to go.

The girls couldn't resist doing a little teasing. As the man started to pass through the front yard, carrying his bundle, one of the Miller Girls (nobody would ever confess as to exactly who) tossed a small stone over the window ledge. The rock barely missed the visitor's heel.

The guest gave no indication that he was the slightest bit aware of the prank. He sauntered on across the yard, headed toward the road.

26

The bit of mischief didn't miss the watchful eye of Mattie. The girls whirled around from their escapade to see their mother sentineled in the door of their second-story room.

"Lawsy, what ya girls think yer doin'?" she exclaimed. "You could'a hit that In-jun. Then what might'a happened?"

The girls suddenly envisioned tomahawks flying through their upstairs window—or three scalps dangling by shanks of red hair, hanging from the clothes line behind their home!

"We're sorry, Mama," they trembled, penitently. "We won't do it again."

They never had another opportunity to resist temptation. The leathery-faced customer who wanted his wife to have one of Miss Mattie's hand-sewn dresses never made a repeat visit to their door.

* * * * * * * * * *

Also, from this same window, the girls could almost detect the outline of the two-story hospital in their community where Mable and Frances had their tonsils removed, without benefit of anesthesia.

Early on the morning of the dreaded operation, Papa had rousted them from sleep and told them it was time to head down the road to Doc Janes' place. All the way, in the wagon, the two sisters debated which one of them would go first for removal.

"You're the youngest. You do it," urged Frances.

"No, you're older than me. You go," relied Mable, tentatively. "If you make it through, I'll know it's OK."

Something about that didn't quite seem fair to Frances, for her to be the guinea pig and all, but in the end, she bravely acquiesced. Mable sat quietly by Papa in the waiting room and listened for any whimper of protest from Frances. There was still time for her to bolt, if she heard Frances being tortured. No sound emerged.

"Maybe this isn't so bad," Mable thought, a little relieved.

After a time, the doctor opened the door and nodded for Papa to help Frances back to the waiting room, while Mable took her turn.

Frances' mouth was packed with gauze, and her cheeks were puffed out like a frog's, so she couldn't give Mable a report of what was to come. Mable saw that her sister was living and breathing, her eyes blinking, so perhaps there was nothing to fear. She soldiered into the room where Frances had just undergone her ordeal. On a linen-draped table lay a hypodermic syringe with a needle as long as an ice pick and an array of mysterious tools that made her flesh creep as she imagined what their purpose might be.

Frances survived this. I can, too, Mable kept reminding herself while she seated herself in the chair and positioned her head for the procedure.

Within seconds, her screams began. Blood-curdling, terrorizing screams that could practically be heard clear back home, where Mama and Bonnie waited for the patients to return. The injection to the tonsils—the only effort available back then for the doctor to use as a pain-killer—hadn't worked on Mable like it had on Frances. Nothing at all went numb in Mable's mouth. She had felt every hellish, agonizing moment as her tonsils were wrenched from her throat.

A horrified Frances and Papa sprang to Mable's side as the doctor opened the door, signaling that the surgery was complete. Like Frances', Mable's mouth was packed with gauze. The two puffy-cheeked sisters rode home in silence.

On that bumpy wagon trip, Mable cast Frances a look suspecting certain betrayal. As soon as Frances could finally muster a few words, she assured Mable, "I never felt a thing. Honest."

None of it mattered when they got home and a sympathetic Mama and Bonnie greeted them comfortingly. Mattie knew just what to do for her girls that afternoon—make some Lemon Ice-Box Pie to soothe their hot, achy throats and to help them put the trauma of the morning behind them.

Neither Red-Haired Miller Girl ever forgot the tonsillecto-my. Nor, for that matter, did Bonnie. Before her sisters' opera-tion, Bonnie heard Papa tell her, "Have one more bout of ton-sillitis, I'll take ya down t' Doc Janes' place, too." But if Bonnie ever took ill with her tonsils again, no one ever knew it. She'd die before she'd let on, after what happened to Mable on that fateful day.

Decades later, on Sunday-afternoon drives around the old home place, Mable could never pass the crumbing walls of the hospital in the country without remarking, "That's where I screamed bloody murder!"

Lemon Ice-Box Pie

1 graham cracker crust
1 (14-ounce) can sweetened condensed
     milk
1/2 cup fresh lemon juice (about 3 fresh
     lemons, squeezed)
1 teaspoon lemon peel
2 egg yolks

Mix all the ingredients and pour into the graham cracker crust. Top with meringue (recipe below).

Meringue:
2 egg whites, beaten until stiff peaks form
     (allow whites to come to room temper-
     ature before beating)
2 teaspoons sugar
1 teaspoon vanilla extract
pinch tartar

Bake in 375-degree oven until meringue is golden brown. Chill in refrigerator.

FIVE

Roll, Jordan, Roll

*

On Sundays, it was never a question of whether the Three Red-Haired Miller Girls would attend church. The only question was where.

Their own church was the New Hope Baptist Church, where Papa was ordained a deacon. It was a considerable distance down the road. On Saturday nights Papa would bring the old Number 3 tub into the kitchen, and Mama heated up water on the stove. With any and all possible menfolk safely shooed away, each of the girls would enjoy the luxury of her weekly bath, so they could be squeaky clean for worship the next day.

Much closer to them was the Methodist church in Brushy Mound. It had beautiful, stained-glass windows, bowl floors, folding seats, and a piano. It was said to be the best rural church in Delta County. If the past week had been rainy, the roads to their church were most likely impassable, so the Miller family became Methodists that weekend. So did many of their good Baptist neighbors. No one thought anything about practicing someone else's religion for one or two Sundays out of the month until the roads ceased to be soup and everyone could proceed on dry ground.

Religion was practiced on more days than Sundays. The girls' Grandma Miller—Papa's mother, Margaret—lived with them for a time, after Grandpa Miller died. The girls didn't acquire as many maxims (you'll read about this in the next chapter) from this grandmother as they had from the colorful Grandma Harris, but one thing they absorbed from her big-time.

The girls would tiptoe past Grandma Miller's room as she readied herself for bed at night. Without fail, they would find her on her knees at her bedside, her head inclined in prayer. The girls never forgot this and learned to follow her example.

In the days before worship became a three-ring circus of multi-media entertainment, as it can be today, Easter pageants were all home-grown. One Easter, Frances and Bonnie portrayed angels at the tomb. Once again, Mattie's seamstress-ship did not disappoint. She made the girls beautiful, gauzy costumes that were light and frothy as whipped cream. Frances thought she might literally ascend into the heavens in hers.

A salesman had just worked the territory around Brushy Mound and had convinced the Miller Girls' church to give a set of Delco lights a try as an alternative to their usual kerosene illumination. The Delco lights were battery powered. Those out on demo to the church were of numerous colors—purples and corals and golds—perfect for an Easter pageant. The glorious Easter morning scene, with the colors of the sunrise breaking behind makeshift props, was so believable, the audience fully expected Jesus to rise, for real, all over again.

A big tabernacle in town was the scene for yearly revivals, attended by people of all faiths, once a year in the summer. These lasted for two weeks, with services twice a day. Everything stopped while the revival was on. From throughout the county families arrived by buggy and wagon. Pallets for babies and sleeping children fringed the tabernacle edges all around.

One year, a minister named Brother Howell was invited to preach the revival meeting. As usual, the visiting preacher was asked to stay with the Millers, since Mattie's cooking was always known to please. Mable was especially excited the year that Brother Howell came, because she had planned to sing with the other young people that formed the revival choir.

When Brother Howell gave his persuasive message and asked those who wanted to respond to come to the front of the tabernacle, Mable left her seat in the choir and went forward, giving her heart to Jesus that night.

One Sunday after church, Mable—along with numerous other neighbors and kinfolk—received their baptism in the local body of water, the gin pool, which of course was next to the cotton gin. All the girls that were candidates for baptism went to some neighbor's house to change clothes. They arrived by the gin pool wearing their baptismal robes. On one side of the gin pool was a grove of willow trees; on the other side, a grassy knoll. Mable thought there surely was never a scene so picturesque this side of heaven.

The gin pool waters may have been less tantalizing than a hot tub, but they were serviceable for the task at hand. Mable, like her sisters had some time before, came up out of the water as a symbol of her decision to follow Christ and climbed the green bank feeling cleansed, ready to walk in a new way of of life.

They would go home to celebrate with one of Mattie's Sunday-dinner feasts, which usually involved fried chicken.

It wasn't until years later, on one of our family's Sunday-afternoon drives around Brushy Mound, that the gin pool got its tag, the "River Jordan." When my mother told me of the outdoor dunkings in her day, all I could think of was Christ being lifted up out of the muddy waters of the Jordan, in the biblical account. To my 10-year-old mind, any outdoor baptistry should have that name. From then on, the label stuck.

More importantly, however, was the decision the Miller Girls made before their trip to the Jordan. I saw the faiths of all three women sustain them through many trials. Each woman would have a husband precede her in death. Repeatedly their belief in an eternal reunion in the presence of the King carried them through each sorrowful time.

And as they themselves began to approach the time when their own days on earth were numbered, none of them expressed fear for the moment they would cross the great Jordan and enter Heaven's Promised Land. They believed in life eternal, and it was enough. It was enough.

Today, the traditional skillet fried chicken of country, Sunday meals has given way to more healthy alternatives. Here's a recipe for Frances' Oven-Crisp Fried Chicken that is a dead ringer for the Sunday fare of yesteryear.

Oven-Crisp Fried Chicken

4-6 boneless, skinless chicken breasts
1 cup all-purpose flour
1 teaspoon salt
1/2 teaspoon freshly ground black pepper
1/2 cup (1 stick) margarine

Preheat oven to 425 degrees. While you prepare to coat the chicken breasts, place 1 stick margarine in a 13-by-9-by-2-inch baking dish and put dish in oven. Heat until margarine melts. In plastic bag mix flour, salt, and pepper. Coat each piece of chicken in this flour mixture. Remove dish of melted margarine from oven and place chicken pieces in dish. Bake at 425 degrees for 30 minutes. Turn chicken pieces. Bake for remaining 30 minutes until chicken is golden brown.

S I X

The Missing Ring

*

The porch swing creaked back and forth, back and forth, as Frances waited patiently. Alternately she watched the horizon and stared down at her ring finger. Still bare, doggone it! She had kicked herself a million times since the day, more than a month ago, when the incident happened that caused her finger to be in its current state.

Frances and her cousins had been playing in the back yard down at Uncle Albert Harris' in Winnsboro. Albert was the big brother of the Miller Girls' mother, Mattie. The girls loved to travel by wagon and see Uncle Albert and Aunt Roxie and their children.

Sometimes Frances and her cousins played Red Rover—a little too roughly for Frances' liking. When they yelled, "Let Frances come over", they linked arms so tightly, it was impossible for her to break through when she ran. The force of their steel-like linkage always threw Frances to the ground. On her last visit there Frances had spent more time shaking the dirt off her from her falls than she did on her feet.

Sometimes she and her cousin Mabel just sat under a big tree in the yard and talked. Mabel was the cousin closest to her age at Uncle Albert's house. On her last visit, Mabel asked to try on Frances' ruby ring. Frances knew she probably shouldn't have worn the ring, which was very special to her, when she went visiting, but she always enjoyed showing it off. After all, she was a teenager now and more given to jewelry and feminine things than she was to acts of her childhood. A boy who was sweet on her had given it to her some time back, and it was her greatest treasure.

Frances wasn't exactly sure how it got away from her—during one of those rounds of Red Rover or when she let Mabel give the ring a try while they were deep in conversation. All Frances knew was that on her way home that she discovered it—her ruby ring was no longer on her hand!

"Please look for my ring," begged Frances, dashing off a letter to her Winnsboro cousins as soon as she returned home. Every day since, she waited for the mail delivery, hoping it would arrive. Secretly, though, she held out little hope because heavy rains had poured several times since the visit to Winnsboro.

At last in the distance she saw it—the bobbing on the horizon of Mr. Wheeler's mail wagon. Vas Wheeler had been their mail carrier for several years now. He came out from Cooper, nine miles away, to deliver the mail. He always stopped and visited with the family when he brought the mail. He sometimes talked about his own family—his wife and his two boys, who were slightly older than Bonnie. As soon as Frances wrote the letter to Winnsboro, she had taken it out to Mr. Wheeler and told him of her plight. He sympathized with her and assured Frances he'd be on the lookout for a return letter or—even better—a package.

As soon as she could make out the outline of Mr. Wheeler's face, she saw it shake a "No" in her direction.

"I'm sorry, Frances," he said regretfully as he moved nearer. "Nothing today, still." He paused his buggy on the road in front of their farmhouse. The rich Delta County dirt that made farming so fruitful always turned the roads sticky and gummy after a rain. Mud was now clumping around the spokes of his wagon wheels, and Mr. Wheeler rested his team for a spell while he picked up a stick from the road and poked the mud out. Frances grabbed a stick herself and helped the older gentleman.

"Thanks, Frances," he nodded to her kindly. "Don't give up hope. These things happen."

Frances nodded and tried to keep a stiff upper lip. She returned to the house to help fix supper. Tonight they were having Buttermilk Pie, one of her favorites. Maybe the delicious flavor of the smooth, creamy custard would be soothing and help ease her heartbrokenness. She helped Mama beat the eggs for the pie.

The next day Frances and her sisters were out in the fields, picking cotton. Delta County was, at that time, part of the most productive cotton-growing region in the world. Entire families were mobilized to pick the crop. On this day Frances was part of the labor force. She had her head bent intently over her cotton sack when she heard Mable call, "Mr. Wheeler! Mr. Wheeler!" Frances looked up to see their carrier pulling his familiar mail wagon to the side of the road, climb down, and proceed down one of their cotton rows.

Frances knew exactly what that meant. Her heart somersaulted big time. In a flash she threw her sack down and blitzed down the field to meet her friend.

"It's my ring! I know it is!" she yelled as she watched Mr. Wheeler waving a small brown box as he walked briskly.

"Special delivery for you, Frances," he called cheerfully. "It just may be what you're looking for." The return address said, "Winnsboro."

Frances yanked on the white twine that tied up the brown paper wrapping. With shreds of paper flying to the ground, she lifted the top and pulled out a matchbox stuffed inside. Deep in the folds of the tissue paper lining the matchbox was

a tiny band of gold, with a ruby set on top. Her ring was back
again!

Excited as everything, the often-reserved Frances jumped
up and gave Mr. Wheeler a hug.

"There, there," he responded paternally, patting her on the
back. "See, I told you. Don't ever give up hope."

Frances wore the ring back to the house but then tucked it
in her dresser drawer before she sat down for dinner. She
wouldn't take any more chances now that the ring was back
safe and sound. All during dinner Frances was smiling—and
not just because of the tasty Buttermilk Pie, which they
enjoyed for a second night in a row.

In days to come, the family of the Three Red-Haired Miller
Girls would grow to link in another special and permanent
way with that of kindly Mr. Wheeler, the mail carrier. But for
Frances, the best memory of all remained the day he made a
special-delivery trip to the cotton field to return the ruby ring,
once thought lost, to her. She kept it safe from then on.

Buttermilk Pie

3 eggs, beaten
2 cups sugar
2 tablespoons cornstarch
1/2 cup (1 stick) margarine, melted
1 tablespoon lemon flavoring
1 teaspoon vanilla extract
1/2 cup buttermilk

Mix ingredients thoroughly and pour into a
9-inch unbaked pie shell. Bake for 350
degrees for about 40 minutes.

S E V E N

Walking Papa Home

*

Mable drifted from room to room, touching the walls, pressing against the windows, memorizing each detail that soon would be part of her life no more.

The time had come for the Three Red-Haired Miller Girls to leave the country. Mattie had made up her mind. Her daughters needed a better education than what the rustic, two-room school house in Brushy Mound could give.

Not that there hadn't been good times there. Growing suddenly misty eyed as she thought about the only life she'd ever known, there in the country, Mable remembered with pride the Friday afternoons when pupils from both rooms combined for a spelling bee. How proud she was when, week after week, her sister Frances was always one of the last two standing, the others having been stumped by a word long before.

Other pictures flooded her mind—one of the wide ditch, just south of the school. On cold, winter days when it was dry and the sun out bright, the Three Red-Haired Miller Girls would sit with their backs to the protective bank of the ditch and eat lunch—usually peanut butter and crackers, with scrumptious fudge packed between crackers for dessert. It was just like Mama to make everyday things seem special, even in stocking their lunch pails.

Where Mama really shone, however, was fixing the girls up for the annual community basket supper. Girls in attendance brought beautifully decorated, handmade baskets. A boy would buy his best girl's basket so he could eat with her. Bidding was sometimes fierce and competitive, and the baskets created by Mattie for her girls often took some of the highest bids.

One year Mattie made a basket into a touring car and another into a train coach, with fried chicken and a slice of Osgood Pie in each. When Frances wasn't looking, a prankish cousin stashed a piece of corn bread and onion in her car, much to her surprise. Mable chuckled to herself in remembering how the lucky bidder on that car got more meal that he was bargaining for.

Nostalgia aside, Mattie had decided it was time for her family to be on the move. Bonnie and Frances were in the older grades now and would still have a few years to benefit from a higher caliber of education than the Brushy Mound school afforded. Mable was in the sixth grade and had a goodly chunk of her learning ahead of her. The schools in town were what they all needed, Mattie told her husband, Mark.

The girls' Papa agreed. Farming was a hard lot in those days, and he begged for a rest from the drudgery. Jobs in town didn't depend on the whims of nature, as did living off the land. Cooper, nine miles to the southwest, represented more stability. So, the Millers were set to go.

As Mable mulled over the idea of living in Cooper, thoughts of the annual county fair she had attended there since she was a child always came to mind. Much like the annual revival in Brushy Mound, the fair was one of the biggest events around their community. Mable, Bonnie, and

Frances could hardly wait to make the trip to town by buggy and to see what delights each year's fair would bring.

Just before fair time, when Mable was 5, Mattie had sewn for Mable a beautiful, blue silk dress, to be reserved strictly for Sundays and special occasions. Mable couldn't wait for Sunday to roll around.

"I have to wear it NOW, Mama," she had begged as Papa hitched up the horses to go to the fair. After all, church happened every Sunday, but the fair came around only once a year. Wasn't that TRULY a special occasion? she reasoned.

"Naw, chile, you'll spill somethin' on it and ruin it," Mattie cajoled. "Then you'll never be able to wear it t' church."

"Mama, I won't. I promise." Mable was in tears now, refusing to be consoled. "My dress is special," she stomped. "I want to wear it today."

Aunt Alice Harris, wife of Mattie's oldest brother, Charlie, happened to be visiting the Miller family that day when the issue about the dress came up. The older woman pulled Mattie aside and wisely advised, "Wrap up the dress and take it with you in the wagon. Tell Mable to wear something else, and she can change dresses when she gets to the fair. She'll be so excited, she'll forget all about it."

Aunt Alice had called it correctly. As soon as the Millers turned into the fair grounds, Mable and her sisters spotted the ring-toss game, among other enchantments.

"Papa, Papa," Mable cried. "Go get in line at the ring toss and win us somethin'." Mable and her sisters trailed after Papa.

The sky-colored dress that Mattie had brought along was not mentioned again that day, just as had been predicted.

Mable was far too excited about the little stemmed juice glass that Papa won for her when his lucky ring slipped surely over the bottle top to even care about anything else.

One day, when she would grow up and no longer drank juice from it, she would give it to her little girl, who drank juice from it until she was grown and then gave it to her little girl to drink juice from. It would always be a reminder of the Delta County fair and the day that the blue silk dress totally slipped Mable's mind.

* * * * * * * * * *

The move to Cooper meant an entirely new set of diversions. The Sparks Theater on the square was like nothing the Miller Girls ever experienced in Brushy Mound. The family went every Friday night to the movies. The theater showed a continuous film along with the main feature, a way of insuring a full house.

One day a new movie entitled "The Red-Head" starring Clara Bow came to the Sparks. Mable, along with all the other redheads in the Cooper schools, got free admission to the movie. Despite the teasing she sometimes endured because of her carrot top, Mable saw that it paid to have a head that stood out from the crowd.

After their schooling was over, Bonnie went to work for a dry goods store; Frances became secretary to the mayor of Cooper and later worked at the First National Bank, and Mable held jobs at the local dry goods as well as at Perry Brothers Variety.

When the day's work let out for Mable, she met up with Papa, who had found work at the local lumber company when the family moved to Cooper. Having Papa along as a companion made the walk home more pleasant. They talked about their work day and mused over what Mama might have on the table for them to eat for supper.

As the days wore on, Papa's pace slowed. Mable, with youthful spring in her step, found it difficult to hold back to match his plodding.

His breath began coming in short staccatos. Sometimes he had to stop and prop against some resident's picket fence until he got a second wind.

Mable grew worried. "Papa, what's wrong? Do I need to go for help?"

"Jest not as young as I use t' be," he sputtered, straightening himself and trying to minimize what ailed him. "Go on home and help yer Mama with supper. I'll be 'long soon."

"Papa, I want to stay here with you. I don't mind waiting. Honest I don't."

Papa held firm. "Tell yer Mama I'm on my way." So Mable sped along.

Papa continued with labored steps until at last he reached the house. He downed his dinner and quickly collapsed into bed for the rest of the night.

And so it went, one work day after another—Papa and his youngest walking together for a while and then parting company, with Papa insisting that his daughter quickly make her way ahead of him.

One weekend, with work behind him, Papa went to bed and never got up. When the doctor was called, he pronounced Papa's heart to be in a greatly weakened state. Breathing was raspy and ponderous. Each day over the next several, he lost more ground.

Finally, with those Papa loved gathered around him, his eyes closed to open no more. As Mark Miller lay in state in his casket, many said how incredible it was that a man of 51 could still have such hair of flame, that family trait from which his three daughters drew their trademark tresses.

The Three Red-Haired Miller Girls mourned for their Papa. In Mable's mind for many decades bubbled regret over all those evenings she had raced along from work instead of staying behind to walk Papa home.

Gradually, as the days passed, the business of mourning was put behind them. The girls stolidly turned their attentions to their widowed Mama and linked their resolve to do what they could to help. Bonnie apprenticed under Mattie until she acquired all her sewing skills. The two of them took in as much work from the public as they could to support the family. Frances and Mable pitched in part of their wages to help make a way.

Their stress-filled life in town seemed long removed from the days of blissful basket suppers and spelling bees and two-week-long tabernacle meetings that once had been so much a part of them.

It wasn't too many years until the call to a rural existence beckoned again. Bonnie and her husband, Bill, took up life on a picturesque little farm, in a white frame cottage just a few miles from Bonnie's old Brushy Mound homeplace.

Another generation of Miller-Harrises had returned to country roots once more.

Osgood Pie

1/2 cup (1 stick) margarine
1 cup sugar
2 eggs, beaten
1/2 cup raisins
1 cup pecans
juice of 1/2 lemon
1 baked 9-inch pie shell

Melt margarine. Add sugar, eggs, raisins,
pecans, and lemon juice. Cook over medium
heat until thickened, stirring constantly. Pour
into baked pie shell.

SEVEN

The Four Peas

*

Grandma Harris was greatly beloved by her 11 children who lived to adulthood and by her 57 grandchildren, so much so that "Grandma Harris" maxims trickled down to many generations.

I was put to bed at night with one such "Grandma" saying ringing in my ears: "If you get hot in the night, don't throw off the quilt, or you'll catch cold. Instead, just stick a foot out from the cover, and it'll cool your whole body." It's an admonition that my own children (Grandma's great-greats) can also recite practically by heart.

One day news came to Grandma's loved ones that their matriarch had fallen and broken her hip. She was 81. The doctor declined to do surgery, saying she was too old to undergo it. One of the kinfolks took a kitchen chair and put wheels on it so Grandma would have a way to get around, since she could no longer walk because of the injured hip.

Because everyone was so concerned about Grandma, all the relatives came from miles around to check on her. Grandma's children and their children and even their children all gathered at the same time to let Grandma know they cared about her. Everyone brought food for a big family dinner. Home-cooked dishes of all kinds abounded. Folks were hungry from traveling and visiting, so they dined with immense appetites. The adults loaded up their plates, followed by the younger set. The older children pushed in line first, of course. That left the smaller ones as the last to be served.

By this time in her life, Bonnie was the mother of Yvonne, who at age 4 was one of the youngest in the crowd. Yvonne brought up the rear in the serving line. By the time she reached the spread, all that remained for her to put on her plate were four peas!

For many years later, even when she herself was a grandma, family members retold to Yvonne the story of the day she ate the four peas for dinner. (Yvonne went on to become an excellent cook, especially of recipes involving vegetables, such as this Squash Dressing that follows.) Who could blame her? Perhaps that was one way to ensure she'd always have some for herself!)

And Grandma Harris went on to live 11 more years, all of them spent in her makeshift wheelchair because the doctor refused to set her broken hip. Surprisingly, in photos of Grandma in those later years, she always wears the sweetest, most peaceful smile despite her hardship—a true example of patience and forbearance.

Squash Dressing

4 cups cooked squash
1 (10 3/4-ounce) can cream of chicken soup
1 large onion, chopped
1 (2-ounce) jar pimientos, chopped
1/2 cup (1 stick) margarine, melted
1 teaspoon salt
1 (6-ounce) box corn bread stuffing mix

Mix all ingredients and pour unto greased
13-by-9-by-2-inch baking dish. Bake at 350
degrees for 30 minutes. Serves 8-10.

NINE

Sunday Dinner
and the Dime-Store Dishes

*

When the venerable Mr. Wheeler had visited the Red-
Haired Miller Girls on his mail route and told them about his
two sons, the brothers of whom he spoke could not have been
any more unalike than if they had been lard and molasses.
They were born to the same mother and father, and both
entered the same line of work—their father's profession of
the postal service. There, the similarity ended.

Mr. Wheeler's firstborn, H.B., or Buford, was somewhat
slight of build and fair, with his mother's penchant for poetry
and music and a yen to see the world. And he got to. Early
on, he moved out of Cooper to the big city of Dallas, joined
the post office there, married a Dallas girl, and eventually
shipped off to Europe, where he helped run the military post
office in Germany after World War II. Occasionally a wonderful package bearing interesting, foreign stamps arrived at the
Cooper post office for Mr. Wheeler to bring home to his wife,

Zella. It contained cuckoo clocks or Meisen china or other novel bric-a-brac that Buford sent back to his mom.

That left Mr. Wheeler's younger son, J.D., or Doyce, back home as Cooper's most eligible bachelor. Sometimes known as "Jelly" because of his dapper, slicked-back hair that must have reminded some of a shiny jelly bean, Doyce was dark, robust, and hardy, with a football-player build and as strong a yen for the home front as his brother had wanderlust. Until his senior years, people recalled the day that Doyce Wheeler struck a hole-in-one on the Cooper golf course. All the girls wanted a date with this local celebrity.

The lucky one snared him after friends paired them up on a blind date for a Fourth of July picnic. "Jelly" Wheeler got hooked up with none other than Little Red, the youngest of the Three Red-Haired Miller Girls. Mable's bright auburn tresses and friendly smile caught his eye. They dated from then on. Because she was seven years his junior, Mable had only known J.D. from a distance before then, even though they both grew up in the same small town.

Even at that, it took J.D. seven years to get around to pop The Question. Thoroughness and discretion were his lifetime trademarks. The marker over his grave today contains an inscription from I Corinthians 3:11: " For other foundation can no man lay than that is laid, which is Jesus Christ" (KJV). J.D. wanted a firm foundation for everything he did. Getting ready for marriage was no exception.

During her seven years of waiting, Mable had plenty of chances to eat Sunday dinner with the Wheeler family after church. While preparing lunch alongside her future mother-in-law one Sunday, Mable heard Zella remark, "Oh, don't leave so much potato on the skin when you peel it. There won't be enough potatoes to mash if you do it that way." Tiny Zella, who barely came to 5-foot-3-inch Mable's shoulders, wanted to be sure her boy would have enough potatoes to eat once he was a married man. Mable monitored every potato peel from then on.

However, the state of the potatoes—or anything else served, for that matter—was scarcely noticed because the table setting at the Wheeler dining table was so spectacular. On a red-and-white checked cloth was placed a set of dishes in brilliant colors—cobalt blue, medium green, yellow, orange, and turquoise—a literal fiesta of hues to the eyes. Although they came from the local dime store, they set a table attractive enough for royalty. That's what Mable felt like when she dined there. After all, she WAS a lady-in-waiting. And she waited and waited and waited some more.

Long years later, after J.D. ultimately married his sweetheart, Zella was gone, and Mr. Wheeler disposed of their material life accumulated together, he gave those dime-store dishes to Mable, because he knew how many meals she ate on them. And Mable, because she had plenty of dishes of her own, passed them on to me. They eventually made their way to a storage building in Colorado, where we held items for a cabin we hoped to build someday. That idea proved unworkable, so we sold the land and the shed and all of its contents.

I could hardly get the dishes out of my mind. One day when I walked into an antique store, I saw that one saucer like those from my grandmother's colorful dishes sold for $9.99—what the whole set had cost Zella in the 1930s.

"You parted with your Fiestaware?" the incredulous clerk asked me when I related my story. "Those dishes are *very* valuable these days."

That was all the prompting I needed to get the wheels in motion to bring my set home. Just before the Colorado land deal closed, we paid some college students who were traveling in the area to drive into a remote part of the Rockies and haul those dishes down from the mountain and back to Texas.

Today, on holidays at my house, a 90-year-old Mable sits down to the same vivid, dime-store place settings as she had as a lady-in-waiting. On them is usually served Company Potatoes, the skins having been peeled to ever-so-thin a sliver.

Company Potatoes

8-9 medium potatoes
1 cup French onion dip
1 cup small curd cottage cheese
1 tablespoon margarine
salt and freshly ground black pepper to taste
milk
grated Cheddar cheese
4-5 strips of bacon, fried (or bacon bits)

Peel potatoes, pare, boil, and mash. To
mashed potatoes add dip, cottage cheese,
margarine, and enough milk to make fluffy.
Pour into a greased 13-by-9-by-2-inch baking
dish and top with grated cheese and bacon
(crumbled). Refrigerate until ready to use.
Bake at 350 degrees until hot. If not refrigerated bake 15 minutes in oven or 30-45 minutes if refrigerated a while. Serves 8-10.

TEN

That Little Thing

*

As they stood in front of the mirror and brushed their flame-kissed locks, the Three Red-Haired Miller Girls must have mused many times about the day they would welcome their own little red-haired offspring into the world and pass their most noted feature on to another generation.

It was not to be. Bonnie's daughter, Yvonne, arrived with hair as black as coal. Years later, as each of Bonnie's three grandchildren came into the world, Bonnie carried them one by one out into the sunlight and searched in vain for even the slightest auburn trace. Nothing there.

Frances, although beloved by all her nieces, nephews, and great-nieces and nephews, and looked upon by them as another parent or grandparent, was to have no children of her own.

Nor was Mable to have a child of her flesh and blood. The trademark, paprika-colored mane for which the Three Miller Girls were known, even into their senior years, ceased with them and carried no further into another tier of progeny.

Despite this and other obstacles, Mable's branch of the Miller-Harris line managed to roll on. One day a doctor in Garland, the Dallas suburb where they now lived, telephoned Mable and J.D. He knew that this well-liked couple could not have children born to them but that they wanted to be parents very much. He told them about a baby, to arrive soon, that would need a home. He was caring for a young woman who wanted to make an adoption plan for her child. Would they like to be parents of this baby?

Mable and J.D. excitedly said yes. They headed off to a department store and bought diapers, baby clothes, bottles, a crib, and everything a baby needed.

In a few more weeks, the doctor called again and asked them to meet him at the hospital. Whey they arrived, they saw the doctor walking down the hall, toting an infant.

Gender: Female   Eyes: Hazel

Hair: BROWN Brown! Drat the luck!

Though the candidate lacked the desired carrot top, Mable decided to take her, anyway. The new parents drove away with their new daughter and were very happy.

When they arrived home, Mable said to J.D., "I need to warm her bottle. Would you please hold her?"

J.D. looked puzzled as he gazed at the little brown-haired girl in the pink blanket. "You want me to hold that little thing?" he asked.

But he did learn to hold the small bundle. After lots of warm bottles of milk and a number of years, "that little thing" grew into not so small a person after all.

Perhaps that's why milk, to this day, is my beverage of choice. Maybe, subconsciously, I remember the safety of my Daddy's arms cradling me all those times my mother fixed up her milky brew on the stove.

It seems only fitting to share my recipe for some rich, Velvety Cheese Soup which requires plenty of milk but (a warning here!) which, if heartily consumed, will cause even the most diminutive to be a "little thing" no more.

Velvety Cheese Soup

1/4 cup margarine
1/2 cup finely diced onion
1/2 cup fnely diced carrots
1/2 cup finely diced celery
1/4 cup flour
1 1/2 tablespoons cornstarch
1 quart (4 cups) chicken broth
1 quart (4 cups) milk
1/2 teaspoon soda
1 1/2 cups shredded Cheddar cheese
salt and pepper to taste

Using a large pot, melt margarine. Add
onions, carrots, and celery. Saute over low
heat until onions, carrots, and celery are soft.
Add flour and cornstarch and cook until
mixture is bubbly. Add broth and milk and
make a smooth sauce. Add soda and cheese.
Season with salt and pepper. After pouring
servings int soup bowls, sprinkle top of soup
with parsley and bacon bits.

ELEVEN

The New Cousin

*

Unlike Grandma Harris' gigantic family from which the Three Red-Haired Miller Girls sprang, some branches of the succeeding generations were small in number, at least where my own connection to the family tree was concerned.

Whereas my mother, Little Red Miller, had more first cousins than she could count, I had only one—Bonnie's daughter, Yvonne, who was 18 years my senior and who grew up to marry Joe. Their two children, Mark (named for his Great-Grandpa Miller) and Bill (named for Bonnie's husband), were my childhood playmates. I easily got caught up in their pursuits of making mud pies in the back of my Uncle Bill's pickup truck, playing cowboys and Indians, and a slew of other pastimes that absorbed me thoroughly.

Although I enjoyed hobnobbing with the guys, I soon learned with utter delight that a new baby cousin would be born into their family. I secretly hoped that this new arrival would be a girl and that I would have a cousin of my own gender. All summer before Yvonne's baby arrived, I wrote notes to my friend Nan, guessing whether the baby would be a boy or girl, when it would be born, how much it would weigh, what its name would be.

Also during the summer of that year—1960—the national
political conventions were being held. The big contest for
President was between John F. Kennedy and Lyndon B.
Johnson. My mother and dad were big Republicans and
would never vote for either man. They wanted to see their
fellow Texan, Johnson, nominated because they thought he
would be more easily defeated by the Republican candidate
than would the popular Kennedy. While the convention was
being aired on TV, all over the den of my house were handmade signs that said "Johnson for President" or "All the Way
with LBJ."

On Wednesday night during the week of the Democratic
convention, my mother and I went to church. When we
returned, we immediately flipped on the TV to see what had
occurred. At first we paid no attention to a little yellow piece
of paper that lay on top of the TV set.

After an hour or so, I walked by the TV and tossed a
glance over at the yellow sign. To my surprise, I saw that it
read, "It's a girl. 8 pounds 12 1/2 ounces. Mother and baby
fine." It was in my granddad's handwriting. (My granddad,
of course, was Mr. Wheeler, the mail carrier. My grandmother,
Zella, had recently died, and my granddad lived in a little
house behind us.) He took the message when my mother and
I were gone to church and left the note lying on the TV.

I shrieked for joy, since the sign confirmed that my hopes
for a new baby girl cousin had come true. Then I turned to
my dad, who had returned home before my mother and I, to
ask why he hadn't told us the good news. He replied, "I saw
that piece of paper, but I just thought it was another political
sign for LBJ. I didn't pay it any mind."

The next day, my mother and I journeyed to Cooper to see
the new cousin. When we drove into the yard at Bonnie's, my
two boy cousins came running out yelling, "We have a new
baby sister! We have a new baby sister!"

Of course, with two older brothers, my new cousin Lynda
became just like I had—easily absorbed in their antics and

playing cowboys and Indians and making mud pies in the back of the pickup truck, along with them.

Along the way, Lynda did follow in the tradition of her forebears, the Three Red-Haired Miller Girls, and learned to be a fabulous cook—of more than just mud pies. At our family gatherings, we all call for her dish of Texas Corny Dip, featured on the next page.

Texas Corny Dip

2 (11-ounce) cans shoepeg corn
1 (8-ounce) carton sour cream
1 cup mayonnaise
10 ounces shredded Cheddar cheese
10 ounces shredded Monterrey Jack
    cheese
1 (4 1/2-ounce) can green chilies
1 tablespoon garlic
chopped onion

Mix all ingredients together. Serve with chips
or crackers.

TWELVE

The Great Christmas-Tree Caper

*

If it hadn't been for all the exquisite Christmases in the country that I spent in my growing-up years, the Christmas Tree Caper might have been enough to wipe out my exuberance for the holiday.

Those growing-up Yules were as close to Currier and Ives as you could get, considering the fact that we lived in Texas where snow was rare and considering that our horse-drawn carriage was a '53 Buick.

From the minute we emerged from our over-the-river-and-through-the-woods trip from Garland (or, at least, over the highway and past the town square) and arrived at my Aunt Bonnie's farm house, the stage was set for a delectable day.

As soon as they heard the car tires crunch the driveway gravel, my cousins Mark and Bill raced out to greet us, brandishing their new toy rifles or whatever Santa had brought their way.

But play would have to wait until after I had gone inside and peered under every cake lid and scoped out every dish on the stove. The aromas of Christmas basting and roasting and baking were everywhere. I could hardly wait to see what straight-off-the-farm goodies awaited us on the serving table.

Favorites were Bonnie's Beet Pickles, fried corn, fresh green beans, fluffy mashed potatoes, and squash casserole. In the pastry department were chocolate pie, Osgood pie, orange slice cake, applesauce cake, and buttermilk pie, among others.

Then, once the feasting began, it could never go fast enough, because the Christmas tree that we could observe from the dining room held many delights. How time dragged while the Three Red-Haired Miller Girls washed the dishes (by hand, of course) and the put away the food so we could open presents, or "have the tree," as the older ones always said in country-talk back then.

That's because the gifts that awaited us there were far from ordinary. Most were handmade or handsewn in the past year's burst of creativity that always left me breathless. Almost every Christmas, I found that Nanny (my name for my mother's mother, Mattie) had made an entire new wardrobe for one of my dolls. Often the clothes were cut from fabric that she had used to make some matching dress for me that was also under the tree.

Another year, when Santa had brought me a set of doll beds, she stitched for me a complete set of linens—sheets, pillowcases, blanket, quilt, and bedspread for each twin bed. No decorator room in any home was ever so well outfitted.

Aunt Bonnie's gifts were often of the same ilk. She and Nanny often joined forces to stitch up something special for me. Each family member was treated similarly. Sometimes those gifts of stitchery were reciprocated with handmade things by Mable or Frances. None of the Red-Haired Miller Girls lacked for talent in the creativity department!

When the halcyon day was over, I would ride home with my head literally dancing with sugarplums from the yield of the magical tree at Aunt Bonnie's house.

It was another tree, another time that would almost do me in. It happened the year I was a high-school sophomore. I had just bought my first pair of fashion boots. Women had just begun wearing boots. Mine were quite stylish. I could hardly wait to show them off to my friends.

The occasion soon arose when my high-school choir held its Christmas concert. The director told the choir members to dress casually. On stage were sofas, rugs, a fake fireplace, and a fully decorated Christmas tree. The director wanted the singers to sit around the fake fir and sing their Christmas numbers. I wore my new boots, some new royal blue wool slacks, and gold sweater with royal blue trim.

The choir performance lasted about 45 minutes, during which time I sat on the floor with my feet (and new boots) tucked under me. At the end of the singing, the director motioned for the choir to stand as the audience clapped. When I started to stand, I discovered to my horror that both of my legs had gone totally to sleep. When I tried to rise, it seemed that I was paralyzed from the waist down, since I had no feelings in my legs at all.

As a result, I fell forward. Since I was short and always was stationed on the front row, I fell right into the choir director's stand. The stand with all its music fell backward onto the choir director. As he tried to grab for the stand and the strewn music, he fell backward onto the Christmas tree. The Christmas tree then fell backward, and the glass balls and ornaments on it began to drop from the tree. Several of them rolled into the laps of the front-row audience members.

The audience, instead of being horrified, thought the activity on stage was designed to be a clever ending to the songfest. People in the audience clapped and laughed uproariously. But the choir director wasn't laughing. He was furious with me. Backstage, he yelled at me. "Why did you have to go and ruin a good performance?" he groaned.

But during intermission, people from the audience began slapping him on the back and saying things like, "Great job,

Henderson. You really gave me some Christmas cheer. I don't know when I've ever had such a good laugh." When some people approached him, they still had tears in their eyes from laughing so hard. An audience member said, "One of those balls fell into my lap. I'm going to keep it forever to remember this performance."

The choir director always believed that I ruined his program. He didn't really like being known for slapstick comedy instead of beautiful music. But he didn't fight it when attendance at choir concerts at the high school started growing because everyone came to see what riotous act the choir would pull next.

Beet Pickles

1 gallon beets, quartered
2 cups sugar
1 stick ground cinnamon
3 1/2 cups vinegar
1 tablespoon ground allspice
1 1/2 cups water

Cook beets until tender. Simmer the remaining ingredients 15 minutes. Add beets and boil 5 minutes. Place into canning jars that have been processed in boiling water bath. Seal jars.

THIRTEEN

Tuna Fish
and the Marriage Proposal

*

"Little Red" Miller may have had seven years to think about what she'd say when finally asked to wed, but I, as her daughter, did not have that luxury in the matrimony department.

In fact, when my Prince Charming popped the question, it happened so suddenly and startlingly that I had to discern whether it was an indecent proposal before I gave an answer.

It all started when I, as a student reporter for the campus newspaper at Baylor University, was asked to write a story about a trip to Europe and the Holy Land. A religion professor was planning the trip for students that summer. As I sat in Dr. Hilburn's office and learned about the trip he would lead, I grew eager to be one of the participants and eventually signed up. I returned from the interview and shared the details with Louis Moore, a fellow reporter who was a religion major. He also became interested in going.

In the end, however, Louis got a job that kept him tied to the U.S. for the summer. Since he was fascinated by all the places that our group would travel, he gave me some money and asked me to send him postcards from every stop. As he received my postcards from the month-long journey, he sometimes wrote me back.

Dr. Hilburn, the trip sponsor and a mischievous sort, knew both of us and made a big production whenever he found Louis' letters to me among the envelopes that awaited our group at our various hotel stops. He waved Louis' letters in the air dramatically and made sure that everyone on the trip knew that I had a regular male correspondent.

When I returned to the Baylor campus in the fall, Louis asked me to join him for an evening of showing him my Europe/Holy Land pictures. In looking back, I now categorize this as our first serious date. Other dates followed that fall. I sensed that things were building to a logical conclusion in our relationship, but Louis had mentioned nothing about future plans. He already was accepted as a seminary student in Louisville the following fall, and I was still a college junior.

Remembering my mother's protracted and long-distance wait on my dad, I figured I was in for a similar stint. I wondered whether I needed to learn to crochet to make a bedspread, as she had while she waited seven years for my dad to make up his mind.

However, one night, about four months from the first evening I shared the Europe photos, Louis asked me to visit his apartment to help prepare dinner—one of his typical student-bachelor gourmet creations of tuna fish salad, macaroni and cheese from a box, and green beans from a can. I was doing my part—chopping up pickles at the kitchen sink. Louis was at the stove, with his back to me, stirring the boiling macaroni.

Suddenly, between knife strokes that divided the pickles into neat chunks, I heard this sentence emerge from behind me, "I was wondering how you would like to come with me to Louisville, Kentucky, to live next fall."

I was dumfounded. This swain had his nerve. Any words of commitment or the "L" word—Love—had yet to be mentioned during our four-month courtship. And this question—"come with me to Louisville to live"—what exactly did this mean? As a roommate? As a kept woman? It seemed that a few key words were missing from this inquiry, which sounded a bit more like a proposition than a proposal.

Turns out, what prompted this was a conversation he had engaged in that afternoon with our newspaper advisor, David McHam, who told Louis, by then the newspaper editor, that he was thinking of appointing me as editor for the next fall. Louis quietly panicked, since he had been hatching up other ideas involving me regarding the fall semester—and since the "L" word, indeed, was operative in his thoughts, if not his conversation. At that point, he quickly arranged the tuna fish-macaroni-green bean dinner at his place and popped his details-missing question.

Eventually, that evening, all the lacking parts were supplied. Over the ensuing meal of tuna fish-macaroni-green beans, we planned our future life together, including how I could finish college long-distance as a married woman and work for one of the news organizations in Louisville. Then we visited the home of our newspaper advisor to tell him he'd have to select another to edit his paper for fall. We also visited Dr. Hilburn, who took full credit for planting seeds for our match through his letter-waving antics on the trip. In gratitude, we asked him to perform our wedding ceremony.

That future life together—33 years of it now—has included many other meals of tuna-macaroni-green beans, which we prepare not so much for culinary as sentimental value. Needless to say, our weekly grocery list always includes several cans of tuna fish—the main ingredient in the following Tuna-Fish Casserole, also a favorite.

Tuna-Noodle Casserole

1 small onion, chopped
1/2 small green pepper, chopped
3 tablespoons margarine
1 (10 3/4-ounce) can cream of mushroom
   soup
1 (6-ounce) can tuna, drained
milk
salt and freshly ground black pepper
Worcestershire sauce
1 (8-ounce) package egg noodles
grated Cheddar cheese

Chop onion and green pepper and saute in
margarine in a skillet, until onion and pepper
are soft but not brown. Add soup and
drained tuna. Add enough milk to make a
nice sauce. Season with salt, pepper, and
Worcestershire sauce, to taste. In a separate
pan bring water to a boil and add egg noodles until noodles are cooked. Drain noodles.
In a greased casserole dish, alternate layers
of noodles, sauce, and grated cheese, ending
with cheese. Heat in a 350-degree oven until
the mixture bubbles around the edge (about
15-20 minutes.) Serves 6.

FOURTEEN

One Day in January

*

Once again, years later, the lives of the Three Red-Haired Miller Girls would intersect with the life of that legendary Texan, Lyndon B. Johnson—again, from afar, but powerfully.

One January evening, the eyes of the nation were glued to their television sets to the news that by-then former President Johnson had been stricken with a massive heart attack and had died.

Louis and I were so immersed in following this story that we barely heard the telephone ring in our little Houston townhouse. When the noise finally penetrated our focus on the TV screen, we learned news that caused LBJ's passing to pale by comparison.

"It's your mother," Louis reported to me grimly, his hand over the receiver. "Your Uncle Herbert has just been struck by a train and killed behind his barbecue place in Mesquite."

Over the next few days, LBJ was laid to rest in Texas, complete with the pomp and pageantry and television coverage that accompanies the passing of a chief of state.

But we never saw another frame of news. In fact, the other cataclysmic event that happened on January 22, 1973, when the U.S. Supreme Court upheld *Roe v. Wade* and legitimized abortion on demand, completely bypassed us, too. Several months later, when someone referred to the fact that abortion was legal now, I shrugged and laughed, ignorantly, "It most certainly is NOT! Where did you get that idea?" It took several more weeks and several trips to the *Houston Chronicle* newspaper archives to convince me that this dark occurrence actually happened, as well, on that black January day—making a trio of January 22 tragedies. I had never heard a word about it.

That's because our next hours and days were spent burying a beloved uncle and helping carry Aunt Frances over the tragedy of having her husband of 32 years wrenched from her and our next weeks and months were spent crawling out from under the utter devastation of this powerful life taken from us far too soon.

To this day, whatever caused Uncle Herbert to miss the train at the crossing just behind his barbecue restaurant remains a mystery. He knew that train schedule as well as he knew the innerworkings of the amazing barbecue pit that he patented and that brought customers from all over Dallas to his suburban eatery. Several times a day that train whistle drowned out conversation at his restaurant, where local politicos and power brokers rubbed shoulders with long-distance truck drivers to discuss the fate of the nation over thick slabs of ribs and juicy link sandwiches.

Often, one of us has speculated that since Uncle Herbert's pickup was struck only a few minutes before 6 p.m., just at the time radio stations were breaking the LBJ story, he well could have been stunned by the news and became too distracted to hear the train whistle. LBJ had been bigger than life to Uncle Herbert. The loss of this hero might have stunned him enough to cause him to fail to look both ways on the familiar track.

All I know is that all of us cousins have spent many years and many words trying to recreate the giant of a person that was Uncle Herbert to our children who never knew him or to our spouses who joined the family later. *Trying* to recreate must be underscored, because no photo of him can depict this loveable, lumbering bear of a man with a quick, dry, determined wit and a mind that must have never slept even when he did.

One day I played for my daughter, Katie, a tape from which suddenly blared out Uncle Herbert's gruff, husky voice just as audibly as though he were in the next room.

"So that was Uncle Herbert," she commented. Well, sort of. What a shame that Uncle Herbert could only barely be captured in that snippet of a taped monologue. And what a shame he never knew our little ones. He would have loved them so much—Matthew and Katie and Jarod and Brett and Shelley and Jason and Marleene. The apples of his eye, they would surely have been. Because he and Aunt Frances had no children born to them, he "adopted" the children and in Bonnie's case, grandchildren, of the two other Red-Haired Miller Girls. But the next generation came too late for him to know. Now, he was gone.

In our attempts to picture him for them, we described a self-made man, left by his father at an early age, a born salesman who was always tinkering with things. His first major invention was the automatic juke box—the nickelodeon. Never seen his name—"Oyler"—inscribed on one at any diner you visited? That's because, unfortunately, another inventor got credit because Uncle Herbert didn't jump through the right legal hoops quickly enough.

But on the ashes of this disaster grew the roses of success. Determined to succeed the next time, he soon developed the first electric, wood-fired, indoor barbecue pit—an entirely new way of cooking barbecue. This time, he got that patent so quickly his fingers flew. He had a lawyer, this time, and did everything right.

It worked. Hotels and restaurants around the country wanted the Oyler pit. He prospered and determined to take it a step further, developing it into an outdoor pit for home use. He had plans on the drawing board, cut short by an undetected rain whistle. Had he lived, Uncle Herbert truly would have made it big. Today, barbecue pits all the way to Japan and Eurodisney have the name Oyler written on them, but someone else now holds the patent.

In his memory, no family Christmas is ever observed without a plate full of Uncle Herbert's barbecue, still prepared his way in the restaurant in Mesquite that succeeded his original one by the tracks.

Today, as I serve up my Christmas helping and pour a stream of his tasty sauce over those succulent cuts of meat, if I am quiet and listen hard enough, I can still hear that voice booming, "How ya doin' there, l'il' Kay? Merry Christmas." My heart is touched, and I remember.

Although I can't print Uncle Herbert's patented recipe, I can print another one that our family likes, well, almost as much.

Oven-Bag Brisket

1 (4- to 5-pound) boneless beef brisket,
    trimmed of excess fat
1 pouch dry onion soup mix
garlic powder
freshly ground black pepper
Worcestershire sauce
2 cups beef bouillon
1 tablespoon all-purpose flour

Place 1 tablespoon flour in oven-cooking bag.
Add soup mix. Rub both sides of meat with
garlic powder, pepper, and Worcestershire
sauce. Place brisket in bag in 2-inch deep
pan. Pour broth on both sides of beef. Seal
bag with twist tie and make six slits in top of
bag. Roast brisket at 300 degrees for about 4
hours. Serves 12-15.

FIFTEEN

To Bed with the Chickens and Brainpower

*

Even though Mable had left the farm years earlier, you could still hear the country in her voice, even long after she had grandchildren.

One night, when she was returning to Houston with my son, Matthew, after keeping him for several days, she came out with the rural expression, "Matthew, I'm so tired tonight, I think I'll go to bed with the chickens."

Dead serious, 5-year-old Matthew fired back with a look of concern lacing his brow, "But Grandma, we don't have any chickens!"

His rejoinder could have easily been traced to Matthew's superior intelligence. Early in Matthew's infancy, a very renowned brain surgeon told his parents that Matthew obviously had a lot on the ball, intellectually.

Unfortunately, the doctor delivered his remark in the midst of a very serious situation concerning the actual contents of Matthew's cranium.

On Matthew's one-month pediatric checkup, the physician routinely tape-measured his skull, jotted down some figures, frowned, and cautioned, "We'll have to keep an eye on this. Proportionately, his head is very large for his body."

Although a typical, worry-wart, first-time mother, I shrugged off the comment. "Yeah, well, so is his father's. Big heads run in my husband's family," I replied.

The doctor made no comment but took more notes. At Matthew's two-month checkup, the situation repeated. Tape measure. Big head. More frowns. "This can indicate that the baby has fluid on his brain," the pedi said gravely. "We'll check again at three months, but we may have to refer him to a neurosurgeon."

Worry began seeping in, but my husband and I still believed a logical cause existed. I dug out my husband's baby photo. His head looked just like Matthew's.

At three months, however, the doctor was undaunted. He shipped us off to the neurosurgeon, who said he'd lay odds on Matthew's being hydrocephalic. Uncorrected, this could lead to blindness, retardation, and even death. He'd have to perform more tests, under anesthesia. If the tests proved positive, he'd install a shunt to redirect the fluid from his brain into his stomach.

The family big-head theory? This great Houston specialist acted as though he never heard me but told me he'd meet us two days later outside 'The Skull Room," an operating suite in The Texas Medical Center.

My stomach dropped as my husband and I watched our firstborn, pacifier bobbing in his mouth and his butterfly mobile fluttering over his head, wheeled off to surgery in an adult-sized hospital bed a thousand times larger than his tiny body. We knew that parents of infants before us had sustained scarier times, but to us, it was our biggest life crisis ever. It even overshadowed the stillbirth of the infant that came a year before Matthew. Our luck with having kids seemed abysmal.

"I'll be out in about an hour and a half with the results of the test," the neurosurgeon told us in parting.

Minutes dragged by. The prescribed hour and a half passed. Then two. Then longer. Friends and family stood beside us and held us up. By that point we were sure Matthew had tested positive and had immediately gone on into surgery for the shunt.

Then Dr. Neblett appeared. "Went just great," he chirped as he beamed.

"Went great," I parroted him, woodenly. "You mean the surgery."

"Oh, NO!" he boomed. "There was no surgery. He tested out just fine. Nothing's wrong with him. No fluid at all. Just a lot of brains in there, I guess. *Hyenh, hyenh.*"

I've never hugged a doctor before or since, but I hugged that one. By that point, I was a mess, disintegrating into tears of relief. We carried our baby home that day and didn't mind at all that it took a week for the red Mercurochrome® to wear off from his scalp where they had already painted him up for brain surgery.

I never forgot Dr. Neblett's quip about intelligence. I found it useful to remind Matthew of this at strategic times, especially in junior high when academic interest lagged a bit.

Today Matthew uses his lots of brains to produce beautiful videos that are shown all over the world by the organization which employs him.

But the ultimate demonstration of Matthew's smartness occurred when he married the fabulous Marcie. Now that was some real brainpower!

With Marcie came her family's recipe for Broccoli Salad, which made such a hit with our family that our relatives demand it even on occasions when Matthew and Marcie don't make the family gathering.

Broccoli Salad

1/2 cup mayonnaise
1/2 cup sugar
2 tablespoons cider vinegar
1 bunch raw broccoli, diced
1/2 small onion, chopped
12 slices cooked, crumbled bacon
1 cup sunflower seeds, dry roasted

Make a dressing mixture by combining mayonnaise, sugar, and cider vinegar. Reserve and chill. Toss remaining ingredients. At serving time add dressing mixture to salad ingredients.

SIXTEEN

Thank You, God and Comfort Food

*

Our initial, disastrous attempts at trying to expand the Miller-Harris line by bringing more children into the world, healthy and safe, didn't end with Matthew's head scare.

An unlimited supply of comfort food–not to mention miracles and prayer—was necessary for Matthew's sister, Katie, to be part of our family, as well.

At Matthew's birth I attained a rare and chronic bladder infection that required four surgeries to help correct. In the middle of this, one medical guru pontificated, "If I were you, I'd get out of the baby business right now. In your condition, you can't afford to have other children."

I was so miserable and felt so despairing, I readily agreed. One morning in 1977 I found myself strapped on a gurney, feet aimed toward an operating room door, with a doctor waiting to perform laparoscopic surgery to end my child-bearing function completely.

The doors parted. I glimpsed a green-gowned trio, instruments poised, ready to whack on my body.

Something inside me yelled out, "No way!" I could almost hear my Granddad Wheeler telling me, as he once told Frances about the missing ring, "Never give up hope."

I was groggy from my pre-op injection, but I still managed to instruct the doctor to cancel the surgery. Putting it mildly, the busy and important gynecologist was peeved.

"What does she mean, interrupting my morning?" he stormed to my husband afterward, in the waiting room. "My patients were inconvenienced because of this."

But the decision was the right one. I found a specialist in another city who devoted his entire practice to treating resistant conditions such as mine. In time, he helped me get well completely. Indeed, I never gave up hope, and the Lord gave us another chance at parenthood. By the summer of 1981, Katie was well on her way to joining our family.

Relief, excitement, and anticipation of this new little one infused our days. But at the beginning of my sixth month, so did early labor pains. What would happen now? So much effort to get healed for pregnancy, and now premature contractions. The doctor sent me straight to bed for the rest of my term. I was to lie still as a statue, with bathroom privileges only. If I so much as flickered a muscle, contractions rippled through my body, threatening this new, little life. How would I keep them at bay for three more months, especially with an active, 5 1/2-year-old to parent as well?

The answer came, in part, from meal after meal that arrived at our doorstep. Angels of mercy—from church, from work, from our neighborhood, from family members who helped out—kept us supplied with nourishing food. The dishes they brought helped put meat on Katie's growing bones in utero and gave Louis a tremendous break so he and Matthew were free to care for bedfast me.

One friend brought nothing but vegetables, knowing I needed some balance in my meals. A neighbor offered an especially favorite dish called Chicken-Dressing Casserole. It was so soothing, my ponderous body felt suspended on a cloud as each creamy bite went down.

In the midst of it all, I learned how truly resourceful one could be though immobilized. Though flat of my back, I met a book manuscript deadline, shopped by phone for nursery decor, and conducted newspaper interviews for my job at the

Houston Chronicle so I could stay on the payroll during this unexpected hiatus from work.

And I prayed—I and countless others who also never gave up hope and who asked God to keep Katie safe until she could be born healthy and whole.

In the end, Miss Catharine Moore arrived two days before term—all 7 pounds, 11 ounces of her. Comfort food had helped make her strong and sturdy—and fortified me. I had one of the easiest recoveries imaginable. I felt well enough to run home from the delivery table.

In gratitude, over the years, I have prepared Chicken-Dressing Casserole more times than I can count, for the sick, the bereaved, and for those like me who needed a little hope, simply in the form of a comforting meal.

Chicken-Dressing Casserole

3 pounds chicken breasts, baked and
    shredded
1 (6 1/2-ounce) package corn bread stuffing
    mix
1 (10 3/4-ounce) can cream of celery soup
2 (14 1/2-ounce) cans chicken broth
1/2 cup (1 stick) margarine

Spread cooked chicken bits in a 13-by-9-by-2-
inch baking dish that has been sprayed with
cooking spray. Heat celery soup diluted with
3/4 can chicken broth. Pour soup mixture
over shredded chicken in casserole. In a pan
melt 1 stick margarine; stir in 1 1/4 cups
broth. Use a fork to stir stuffing into this liquid mixture. Cover chicken and soup mixture with dressing mixture. Bake at 350
degrees for 30 minutes. Serves 6.

SEVENTEEN

Forever Summer in the Country

*

At any minute, I expected to see the faces of my children begin appearing on the side of a milk carton—as victims of child neglect. After all, I was depriving them of a country summer experience, and I was awash in remorse over it all.

For me, summers growing up were just like Christmas had been—synonymous with trips to Aunt Bonnie and Uncle Bill's farm. I lived all school year for that final dismissal bell to ring so I could pack my bag to go run barefoot in their grass and let that warm, black, Delta County dirt sift around my toes once more.

I'd be hard-pressed to say which was the best part. Perched on the bed of Uncle Bill's truck, with the tailgate down, making gooey mud pies with my cousins. Discovering that the collie dog had birthed a litter of puppies under the porch steps and naming them and getting to take one home. Sitting on the back porch receiving instructions on how to string garden-fresh green beans and hearing the crisp *snap, snap* of the vegetables thudding into pots we held in our laps. Accompanying Aunt Bonnie into town to the dry-goods store to walk among the wondrous rows of fabric, picking some for the new school dresses she'd sew for me while I was a guest.

Following Uncle Bill to the barn at milking time and listening to the *swish-swash* of the milking machines as he devotedly called each cow by name and guided her into her stall. Late-afternoon trips to the storm cellar, where we'd hear lightning crackle overhead while we sat on benches alongside Aunt Bonnie's colorful storage shelves of canned green beans and beet pickles and jelly. Falling asleep at night counting cars that whirred down the highway in front of their farm house or waking each morning to the sound of the milk truck arriving for last evening's proceeds.

It wasn't just the summer trips that were indelibly etched. Even a Sunday-afternoon visit, when my mother decided it was time to go "up home" to Aunt Bonnie's, was unadulterated delight. Aunt Bonnie, wearing her flower-print dress and starched country apron, appeared on the porch and waved expectantly the first minute that our car tires crunched on the driveway. But always, hugs of greeting had to wait until I ran to the kitchen to look under the cake lid to find that, once again, Aunt Bonnie had made me my very favorite chocolate cake, with frosting so fudgey that it looked and tasted like candy. Although she had grandchildren of her own to spoil, I always felt treated like royalty when I made these country forays. Aunt Bonnie doted on me as a special niece and made sure she had the desserts I liked most when she knew I was headed her way.

After I grew up and married and we brought Matthew into the world, one of my proudest moments was posing all the family on the front porch of Aunt Bonnie's farmhouse and perching him in his stroller in the midst of them. Yet another generation in the Miller-Harris family had come to the country!

But by the time Matthew was old enough to run barefoot in the grass and let the rich, black mud ooze between his toes, my old childhood, country haunt was unavailable to him.

Aunt Bonnie and Uncle Bill had sold the farm. Their declining years made it necessary for them to take up town life and to live closer to my cousin, Yvonne, and her husband, Joe.

If country summers were to be a way of life for Matthew and Katie, we would have to create them for ourselves.

The answer to that dilemma came in the form of a little yellow farmhouse on five acres of land in South Central Texas, in some gently rolling hills that formed the first wave of the picturesque Texas Hill Country.

We restored the 1918-vintage home with an L-shaped front porch, built a white picket fence around the property, and installed a pond and stocked it with fish. We didn't have a dairy barn like Uncle Bill's, but we did acquire two registered Polled Herefords named Victory and Smurfette.

Neighbors came from miles around when Victory gave birth to twin bulls, named Victor and Vincent—a feat unsurpassed in the history of our little country community.

We harvested tomatoes and pumpkins in our garden. Matthew learned to drive by negotiating a riding mower over the five acres of grass. We planted a row of peach trees and watched them grow from seedlings.

We told visiting roughhousers that we'd put them out on the front porch for the wolves to enjoy if they didn't pipe down. (They believed us!)

My kids had a summer country experience, after all. At last I could stop expecting their faces on the side of milk cartons. My goal for their childhoods was accomplished.

I feared what would transpire in their teen years. I braced myself for the day when their schedules were too full with soccer practice and band practice and choir practice and hanging out with friends to want to come away with parents for the weekend to the farm.

Life circumstances took care of that for us. My husband was transferred out of the state, and for the next 12 years we lived away from Texas. It was time to sell the farm that had been the summer playground for our own youngsters. We did so sadly but with contented gratitude for happy country memories that most of their citified friends would never know.

* * * * * * * * * *

On the surface, our lives today bear little evidence of those "way back in the country" ties that so enriched us.

Today, when we take Sunday-afternoon tours around rural Delta County, like those my relatives narrated when I was growing up, there are few, if any, reminders left of those years when the Three Red-Haired Miller Girls rode Little Button over the flower-strewn meadows or when faithful Mr. Wheeler made his special-delivery trip over the muddy, gumbo roads.

The hospital where the Miller Girls lost their tonsils without benefit of anesthesia is long ago torn down. During my childhood, I could still climb through the crumbling remains of the old Miller home and by listening carefully could almost still hear Bonnie and Frances plotting some Saturday afternoon antics for their baby sister. Wind and weather took their toll on those rickety, derelict walls. Some time ago, that structure disappeared from the scene.

The "River Jordan"—the gin pool where the Miller Girls were baptized—today is indistinguishable on the landscape. Only a historic marker indicates the spot where the thriving rural community of Brushy Mound once existed.

Bonnie and Bill's farmhouse, once the scene of so many delectable holidays and family dinners and summer vacations, is also just a memory. A succeeding owner razed the neat, white frame cottage they called home. A new brick one was built facing away from the road.

Uncle Bill's dairy barn, where he called each cow by name to the *swish-swash* of the milking machines, is the only original structure still on the property, but the altered layout of the surrounding buildings gives the place an unfamiliar look as we pass it on the road.

Most of the old ones themselves are gone, too. The grasses on the graves of Grandma and Grandpa Harris, Mark and Mattie Miller, and Vas and Zella Wheeler have been growing for decades.

Herbert, Bill, and my dad, J.D., who once spiritedly discussed the state of the world while leaning against Bill's pristine white fence beside the highway, are probably convening still but do so beside Heaven's green pastures near streets of gold.

Bonnie, the first Red-Haired Miller Girl to depart the earthly circle, fought cancer long and valiantly. Her passing left a profound gap that none can fill.

Even Joe, Yvonne's strong, capable, godly husband— always the first greeter to bound out the door at any family gathering—has left our number, also claimed by cancer far before his time.

As the years go by, our investment on the Other Side grows increasingly. The empty spots at the family dinner table remind us constantly of how much we still miss those who have gone before.

God graciously granted long years of life to Frances and Mable. At 95 and 90 respectively, they have attained the gray-haired "crown of splendor" that the Bible promises to a righteous life (Prov. 16:31). With that crown, however, the red threads among the silver grow fewer as time marches on. One can only imagine their heads of flame that once rivaled the sunrise and turned the heads of many Delta County swain.

Thankfully, the recipes remain. Just the mere aroma of golden Buttermilk Pie, fresh from the oven, or the sight of a freshly minted jar of beet pickles, their amethyst hues catching a beam of the sun, can transport us to a bygone era, and it is forever summer in the country again.

And the family collection grows, as new members are added to the Miller-Harris line by birth or marriage. They and their contributions enrich us and show us that while God takes away, He also gives and gives and gives again.

A sweet reminder of this circle of life occurred one Christmas when Marleene, the pretty daughter of my cousin Mark and the oldest member of the sixth generation down from Grandma Harris, arrived at the family holiday gathering bearing her "Happy Birthday, Jesus" cake.

The recipe was a simple one—a box of store-bought cake mix, a container of store-bought icing, a tube of decorative icing in a contrasting color. The decorative icing spelled out the message, "Happy Birthday, Jesus."

However, this uncomplicated cake was one of the most significant items on the holiday table because through it, Marleene reminded us of the Reason for the Season. Moreover, she helped us remember that the Miller-Harris heritage is not just one of six generations of good food and endearing family tales but also of a heritage in Jesus Christ, so that the ties are never broken and no earthly parting is permanent for those in Him.

Those family gatherings around the table on earth, though sublime, will one day be surpassed at the banquet table of the King! Thanks be to God.

Family Tree
and
Family Album

MILLER-HARRIS FAMILY TREE

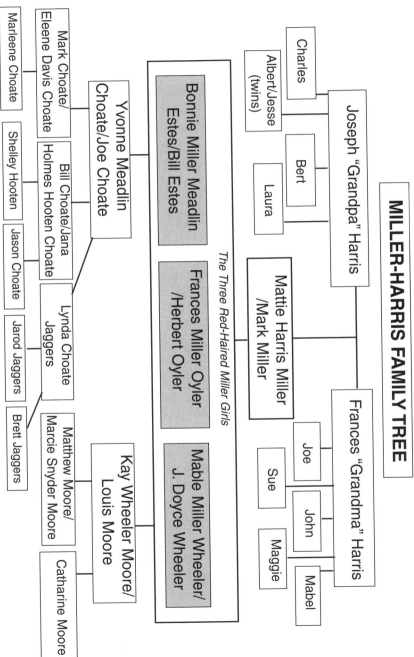

Joseph "Grandpa" Harris

Frances "Grandma" Harris

Charles

Albert/Jesse (twins)

Bert

Laura

Mattie Harris Miller /Mark Miller

Joe

Sue

John

Maggie

Mabel

The Three Red-Haired Miller Girls

Bonnie Miller Meadlin Estes/Bill Estes

Frances Miller Oyler /Herbert Oyler

Mable Miller Wheeler/ J. Doyce Wheeler

Yvonne Meadlin Choate/Joe Choate

Mark Choate/ Eleene Davis Choate

Marleene Choate

Bill Choate/Jana Holmes Hooten Choate

Shelley Hooten

Jason Choate

Lynda Choate Jaggers

Jarod Jaggers

Brett Jaggers

Kay Wheeler Moore/ Louis Moore

Matthew Moore/ Marcie Snyder Moore

Catharine Moore

Family Album

Right—The Three Red-Haired Miller Girls—from left: Mable, Frances, and Bonnie; Below—the Miller home in Brushy Mound before it was razed

Above—Mable on Little Button

Left—Grandma and Grandpa Harris; Above—Mattie and Mark

Vas and Zella;
sons Doyce, left, and Buford

Family Album

Bonnie and Bill

J.D. (Doyce) and Mable

Herbert and Frances

Family Album

Above—Joe and Yvonne;
Right—
7-week-old Matthew meets the
Miller-Harris clan

Joe and Yvonne
with children Mark, Lynda, and Bill and their families

Family Album

The 6th Generation

Marleene   Shelley   Jarod

Jason   Brett

Above—Frances and Mable as
senior members
of the Miller-Harris clan;
Right—Louis and Kay;
Below—Matthew, Marcie,
and Katie

More
Recipes

96

Appetizers and Snacks, Beverages, Jellies

*

Ever get to the mid-afternoon part of a family gathering and catch the relatives drifting back to the kitchen for "just a little bite of something"? These Cheese Balls of Lynda's make a holiday complete after the presents are unwrapped and the frantic rush to catch up on conversation and news of recent months abates a little.

Cheese Balls

2 (8-ounce) packages cream cheese, softened
1 (8-ounce) package Cheddar cheese, grated
1 (2-ounce) jar pimiento, chopped
1 tablespoon chopped green pepper
1 tablespoon chopped onion
1 teaspoon fresh lemon juice
2 teaspoons Worcestershire sauce
dash salt and cayenne pepper
chopped pecans
chili powder, paprika, chopped parsley

Cream cheeses and mix with other ingredients. Form into medium-sized balls. Roll balls in pecans, chili powder, paprika, and chopped parsley. Wrap in wax paper and refrigerate. Serve with crackers.

When my cousin Bill married Jana, he did our family a big favor. Not only is she a delightful person to know, she also brought with her some recipes that were instant hits. Here is her Layered Dip.

Layered Dip

1 (16-ounce) can refried beans
3 avocados, mashed, with fresh lemon juice
　　added
1 (8-ounce) carton sour cream
picante sauce
grated Cheddar cheese
chopped tomato
green onion, chopped

In a rectangular glass pan, layer ingredients in the order listed above, ending with onion. Chill and serve with chips.

Hardly a holiday party has been held at the Moore home over the years without these Cheese Sticks, which make a nice, non-sweet alternative to the trays of cookies we usually also serve.

Cheese Sticks

1 cup (2 sticks) margarine
2 cups grated sharp Cheddar cheese
2 cups grated Swiss cheese
2 2/3 cups all-purpose flour
1 teaspoon cayenne

Soften cheeses, then cream. Add flour and cayenne; blend. Take small pinches of mixture and roll into thin sticks, about 3-4 inches long. Bake on ungreased cookie sheet at 400 degrees for 8 to 10 minutes. Makes 4 dozen.

This Spinach Dip has worked well alongside the Cheese Sticks at holiday party time. It enables guests to get their veggies alongside other treats.

Spinach Dip

1 cup mayonnaise
1 (8-ounce) carton sour cream
1 (10-ounce) package frozen, chopped
   spinach, well drained
1 (1.4-ounce) package Knorr's® vegetable
   soup mix

Mix all ingredients well. Chill until ready to serve. Serve with raw, crisp vegetables.

Lynda shares her recipe for this Carrot Sandwich spread, which she uses as either a thick dip for crackers or vegetables or as a spread for sandwiches.

Carrot Sandwich

2 1/2 cups grated carrots
1 (8-ounce) package cream cheese, softened
1/2 cup chopped pecans
dash of hot pepper sauce
salt and freshly ground black pepper to taste
grated onion to taste
garlic powder to taste
dash of dry mustard
1/2 teaspoon Worcestershire sauce

Mix all ingredients together until well blended. Refrigerate until time to serve.

This Puppy Chow snack has been on many ski trips with Lynda's family and is nice to have around the house during the holidays. It has fed lots of hungry teen-age friends of Jarod and Brett over the years.

Puppy Chow

9 cups of any Chex® cereal
1 cup chocolate morsels
1/2 cup peanut butter
1/4 cup (1/2 stick) margarine
1 tablespoon vanilla extract
1 1/2 cups powdered sugar

Pour cereal into large bowl; set aside. In small saucepan over low heat melt chocolate morsels, peanut butter, and margarine until smooth. Stir often. Remove from heat; stir in vanilla. Pour chocolate mixture over cereals. Stir until all pieces are evenly coated. Pour cereal mixture into a large, resealable plastic bag with powdered sugar. Seal securely and shake until all pieces are well coated. Spread on wax paper to cool. (Avoid using reduced-fat margarine or butter as it may cause chocolate mixture to clump and will not coat the cereal evenly.)

Cucumber Yogurt Dip, on the next page, is great with vegetables as well as chips, crackers, and pita bread. It is nice alternative to the traditional onion soup dip. This dip is especially cool and good in the hot ole summer time.

Cucumber Yogurt Dip

1 pouch onion soup mix
1 cup (8 ounces) plain yogurt
1 cup soup cream
1 medium cucumber, chopped finely
1/4 teaspoon garlic powder
2 dashes red pepper sauce

Blend all ingredients and refrigerate until
serving time.

This Carrot Dip is another light and summery recipe that
uses fresh carrots.

Carrot Dip

3 carrots
1 (8-ounce) package cream cheese, softened
1 tablespoon chopped onion
1 tablespoon Worcestershire sauce
1 shake of red pepper
4 shakes of hot sauce
1/2 teaspoon garlic powder
salt and pepper to taste
1 tablespoon chopped fresh parsley

Grate the carrots by hand or process them in
a food processor. Add remaining ingredients.
Mix well. Chill until serving time. Serve with
vegetables or crackers.

Eleene brought wisdom, humor, and companionship to our family when she married Mark and became a "cousin-in-love". We are thankful for her inclusion of these two recipes, which remind us how much everyone loves Instant Hot Spiced Tea and Hot Chocolate Mix to serve around the holidays.

Instant Hot Spiced Tea

2 cups Tang®
3/4 cups instant lemon tea
2 cups sugar
1 teaspoon ground cinnamon
1 teaspoon ground cloves

Mix well. Use 3 tablespoons mixture in a cup with hot water to make tea.

Hot Chocolate Mix

1 quart powdered milk
1 (1-pound) box powdered sugar
2 tablespoons unsweetened cocoa powder
1 (11-ounce) box Nestle Quick®
1 (11-ounce) jar Coffee Mate®

Mix all ingredients thoroughly. Fill cup 1/2 full with mix. Add hot water and stir.

The recipe on the next page for Sparkling Party Punch has been served at almost every red-letter gathering in the Moore family: Katie's graduation party, Matthew's graduation party, Katie's Sweet Sixteen birthday party, and holiday open houses every Christmas. It makes up quickly and stores in the refrigerator for enjoyment days later.

Sparkling Holiday Punch

1 (46-ounce) can pineapple juice
1 quart cranberry juice cocktail
1 cup sugar
1 cup fresh lemon juice
2 quarts gingerale

Mix the first four ingredients. Just before
serving add gingerale. This recipe makes
from 20-22 servings of punch.

Mable has made this Hot Mulled Cider recipe for many a
Sunday-School class party that she has hosted over the years.

Hot Mulled Cider

1/2 cup brown sugar
1 teaspoon whole allspice
1 teaspoon whole cloves
1/4 teaspoon salt
dash ground nutmeg
1 3-inch stick cinnamon
2 quarts apple cider
orange wedges

Combine sugar, allspice, cloves, salt, nutmeg,
and cinnamon in a percolator basket. Put
apple cider in bottom of percolator and perk
as you do coffee. Serve with orange wedges.
If you want the cider to be the color of tea,
place a tea bag in percolator and let it stay as
long as is required to obtain the desired
color. Makes from 20-22 servings.

This cider of Yvonne's has greeted us at family Christmas celebrations in recent years. It's wonderful to fellowship with a cup of this good, warm stuff in hand while dinner preparations are being finalized and lots of good catch-up conversation is occurring.

Hot Cider

6 quarts apple cider
1/2 teaspoon ground nutmeg
3/4 cups sugar
2 teaspoons whole cloves
few sticks cinnamon

Combine cider with other ingredients and bring to a boil. Boil about 5 minutes; strain and serve. Serves 48.

Baylor University has become the college of choice for several of our family members. This recipe for Baylor Julep appears here in tribute to that alma mater.

Baylor Julep

1 (6-ounce) can frozen orange juice concen-
    trate, thawed and undiluted
1 (6-ounce) can frozen pink lemonade concen-
    trate, thawed and undiluted
1/2 (46-ounce) can pineapple juice
water to taste

Combine first 3 ingredients, mixing well. Add water to dilute to taste. Yield: about 1 1/4 quarts.

NOTE: This is versatile: try with gingerale, fresh fruit, or maraschino cherries.

This punch was served at Mable's 90th birthday celebration, which was held in the fall. The bronze color works well with autumn decorations.

Tangy Party Punch

1 small can lemonade
1 (46-ounce) can unsweetened pineapple juice
1 (32-ounce) bottle Sprite®

Mix lemonade according to directions on can.
Add other ingredients. Chill and serve.

At the other end of the spectrum are these two punch recipes, which lend themselves to summer gatherings.

Summer Punch

2 (12-ounce) cans Orange Plus®
1 (.14-ounce) package strawberry Kool Aid®
1 cup sugar
1 (46-ounce) can pineapple juice
2 quarts water

Mix Orange Plus according to directions on can. Add Kool Aid, sugar, pineapple juice, and water. Mix and chill. Serves 18-20.

Grape-Apple Cooler

6 scoops lemonade flavor drink mix
6 cups white grape juice
2 1/4 cups apple juice
1 (12-ounce) bottle club soda

Combine first three ingredients. Chill. Add club soda just before serving. Garnish with lemon.

Jellies and preserves are an indelible part of country cooking. For years I watched as my Aunt Bonnie brought in the yield of the harvest and put it up for the family to enjoy months into the future. When Louis and I began to replicate those bygone years with our own little farm, we harvested pumpkins galore and turned them into this delicious Pumpkin Butter. We brought it as gifts to the family.

Pumpkin Butter

6 pounds fresh-cooked pumpkin
2 tablespoons ground ginger
2 tablespoons ground cinnamon
1 teaspoon ground allspice
5 pounds light brown sugar
5 lemons
1 pint water

Peel pumpkin. Chop fine or put through food chopper (measure 6 pounds). Add spices and sugar with lemon juice and rind (which has been put through food chopper). Let stand overnight. In morning, add water. Boil gently until vegetables are clear and soft and mixture is thick. Pour into sterilized jars and seal while hot.

Microwave Pumpkin Butter

1/4 cup dark brown sugar
2 tablespoons granulated sugar
1/4 cup water
1/2 teaspoon each ground allspice and cinnamon
1/4 teaspoon each ground ginger, cloves, nutmeg
1 1/2 cups fresh-cooked pumpkin

Combine sugars, water and spices in 4-cup glass measure. Microwave 3 minutes on high. Cool and refrigerate. Makes 2 cups.

Yvonne has delighted all the family by sending us home at Christmas with gifts of Apple or Pear Butter. The unbelievably simple recipe below can be adapted either for apples or pears and makes the most wonderful, smooth spread for biscuits or muffins or toast.

Apple (or Pear) Butter

Cook fruit in small amount of water (enough to prevent sticking) until soft. Amount of fruit you use depends on how much of the butter you desire to make. Mash fruit thoroughly or put through a sieve. Add sugar to taste (usually 1 to 2 cups sugar to 4 cups cooked fruit.) Cook together until thickened. Add cinnamon and cloves to desired taste. Pour into hot jars and seal immediately.

Eleene's own sweet mother, Opal Davis—another of those great, East Texas country cooks—is the source of this recipe for Fig Preserves, which Eleene has given our family as a Christmas treat.

Fig Preserves

7 cups fresh figs, diced
4 cups sugar
1 cup Karo® syrup
1/2 cup water
1/2 lemon, sliced

Bring sugar, syrup, water, and lemon slices to a boil. Add figs, small amounts at a time. Cook until syrup begins to thicken. Remove from heat, pour mixture into jars, and seal.

Salads

*

When it comes to salads, kids (and grown-up kids, too) can be pretty picky. But Aunt Bonnie knew the trick with Bing Cherry Salad. The fact that it contained Coca-Cola® made it doubly appealing to the younger set. This was a festive holiday favorite for many years.

Bing Cherry Salad

1 (15-ounce) can Bing cherries, pitted
1 cup crushed pineapple
2 (3-ounce) packages cherry-flavored gelatin
2 cups juice (from drained cherries)
2 (8-ounce) bottles Coca-Cola®
1 cup chopped pecans

Drain juice from cherries and pineapple to get 2 cups juice. Add water if needed to make this amount. Bring juice to boiling and pour over Jello. Stir until completely dissolved. When cool, add Coca-Cola®, stir, and chill in refrigerator until partly congealed. Add drained cherries, pineapple, and pecans; pour into mold that has been rinsed in cold water. When firm, unmold on salad greens and serve. Serves 8-10.

Frances' Cranberry Gelatin Salad has been the way we've "gotten our cranberries" for many years. The white grapes make it doubly yummy.

Cranberry Gelatin Salad

 1 quart whole cranberries
 3 1/2 cups boiling water
 2 cups sugar
 2 tablespoons unflavored gelatin, soaked in
   1/2 cup water
 1 cup chopped pecans
 1 cup pineapple chunks
 1 cup white grapes

Cook cranberries in boiling water; put through strainer. Add sugar. Dissolve gelatin in cold water; then add it to first mixture. Let stand until cool. Add pecans, pineapple, and grapes. Pour into bowl or into molds. Serves 8-10.

Pretty and pink, this next recipe, Bonnie's 7-Up® Gelatin Salad, has applesauce as an added zinger to make it kid-friendly.

7-Up® Gelatin Salad

 1 (16-ounce) can applesauce
 1 (3-ounce) package raspberry-flavored
   gelatin
 1 (8-ounce) bottle 7-Up®

Heat applesauce in a small pan. Add 1 small package raspberry-flavored gelatin. Cool and add 1 small bottle 7-Up® . Jell. Serves 6-8.

This recipe for Glazed Fruit Salad started making the rounds in our family some years back and spread like wild-fire among all our friends and acquaintances. After Yvonne introduced it, it quickly became the most talked-about item at potluck suppers or church socials. All of us field calls regularly from people asking, "Will you tell me how to make that fruit salad?"

Glazed Fruit Salad

    1 can each pears, peaches, apricots,
        pineapple chunks
    2 medium-sized bananas
    1 (1-ounce) package lemon instant pudding
        mix

Drain juices of canned fruit. Chop up fruit. Cut up bananas. Mix together. Stir in pudding mix. Chill. Serves 8-10.

Jana's recipe is a slight derivation of this delicious dish. Hers is made with peach pie filling.

Peachy Fruit Salad

    1 pint whole fresh strawberries
    3 medium-sized bananas, sliced
    2 (11-ounce) cans mandarin oranges
    1 (20-ounce) can pineapple chunks
    1 (20-ounce) can peach pie filling

Slice strawberries. Mix with sliced bananas. Drain oranges and pineapple and mix in. Stir in peach pie filling. Chill. Serves 8-10.

112

Bonnie's Imperial Salad Freeze always seemed like dessert because it was so sweet and fruity and cold. The cherries and pineapple made it colorful. To a child, it seemed almost like cheating to be able to eat something so sweet earlier than the dessert course.

Imperial Salad Freeze

2 large ripe medium-sized bananas
3/4 cup sugar
1 (8-ounce) can crushed pineapple, drained
2 tablespoons fresh lemon juice
2 tablespoons chopped maraschino cherries
2 (8-ounce) cartons sour cream
1/2 cup chopped pecans

Mash bananas and blend in other ingredients. Stir well and pour into tray or salad mold and freeze until firm. Cut in squares or wedges and serve on salad greens.

Eleene has added numerous yummy dishes to the family holiday food table. This Fluffy Cherry Salad is pretty to look at as well as good to eat. It just looks like Christmas.

Fluffy Cherry Salad

1 (14-ounce) can sweetened condensed
   milk
1 (20-ounce) can cherry pie filling
1 (8-ounce) can crushed pineapple, drained
1 (16-ounce) container whipped topping
1 cup chopped pecans

Mix thoroughly and chill. Serves 8-10.

Lynda obviously inherited her mother's skills as an accomplished cook. Strawberry Pretzel Salad is a dish with surprises—dig deeply enough and you'll find a crust of pretzels. Like Imperial Salad just featured, it could easily fall into the dessert category, as well.

Strawberry Pretzel Salad

2 1/4 cup broken pretzels
3 cups (1 1/2 sticks) melted margarine
1 (6-ounce) package strawberry-flavored
    gelatin
2 cups boiling pineapple juice
2 small packages frozen strawberries
1 cup sugar
1 (8-ounce) package cream cheese
bowl of prepared whipped topping

Mix pretzels and margarine. Put in 13-by-9-by-2-inch baking dish that has been sprayed with cooking spray and bake in 400-degree oven for 10 minutes. Cool. Dissolve strawberry gelatin in boiling pineapple juice. Add strawberries and let set until it begins to jell. Mix sugar and cream cheese. Stir in whipped topping. Combine and put over pretzels. Pour strawberry mixture over topping. Cut into squares to serve. Serves 12-15.

Even die-hards who otherwise won't touch veggies have warmed to this Marinated Vegetable Salad (next page), which Yvonne got us hooked on some years back. Besides being great to taste, it keeps in the refrigerator for days. If you take this to a family gathering or to a covered-dish event, this is guaranteed to be the first dish consumed, down to the very last morsel of shoepeg corn. You'll not bring any leftovers home with you! This is followed by her Apricot Delight Salad, which lives up to its name of being truly delightful.

Marinated Vegetable Salad

1 (15-ounce) can each English peas, French-
style green beans, and 1 (11-ounce) can
shoepeg corn
1 (2-ounce) jar pimiento, chopped
1 small green pepper
4 fresh green onions with some tops
1 cup chopped celery
3/4 cup vinegar
1 cup sugar
2/3 cup vegetable oil
1/4 cup water
1 teaspoon salt
dash freshly ground black pepper

Drain vegetables and mix. Chop green pepper, green onions, and celery. Add to vegetable mixture. Bring to a boil the vinegar,
sugar, oil, water, salt, and pepper. Pour over
vegetables, mix, and let marinate in refrigerator for several hours. Serves 8-10.

Apricot Delight Salad

2 (3-ounce) packages apricot gelatin
2/3 cup sugar
2/3 cup water
2 (4 3/4-ounce) jars baby food apricots
1 (20-ounce) can crushed pineapple
1 (14-ounce) can sweetened condensed milk
1 (8-ounce) package cream cheese, softened
1 cup pecans

Combine gelatin, sugar, and water. Boil to
dissolve; remove from heat and add fruit.
Combine milk and cream cheese and beat
until smooth. Add gelatin mixture and
pecans. Chill. Yields about 20 servings.

I learned to make Bean Sprout Salad at some of the delicious, bring-a-dish salad lunches that we enjoyed in the break room of the *Houston Chronicle* during the years Louis and I worked there. After I perfected it, I shared it at our family gatherings.

Bean Sprout Salad

1 bunch spinach
4 green onions, sliced thin
1 cup bean sprouts
1/2 cup chopped almonds
8 slices bacon, fried and crumbled
1/4 cup vegetable oil
1/4 cup vinegar
2 tablespoons ketchup
2 hard-boiled eggs, chopped
salt and freshly ground black pepper to taste

Wash spinach. Remove stems and tear leaves into salad-sized pieces. Slice onions and toss them along with bean sprouts, almonds, and fried and crumbled bacon with spinach. Blend oil, vinegar, ketchup, eggs, and salt and pepper to make dressing. At serving time toss with salad. Serves 10-12.

As I mentioned in the tale about "That Little Thing", family for me has come in a variety of packages, beyond simply the Miller-Harrises of whom you read here. When I was an adult, I had the privilege of meeting several members of my birthfamily, to whom I was connected genetically and separated from through adoption. With that union have been passed on to me several family recipes, as well. Here is a recipe for Boiled Dressing for Potato Salad from Amanda Elvira Prickett, who was my birth great-grandmother, on the same strata of forebears as Frances "Grandma" Harris in my adoptive family. This makes a creamy dressing that is wonderful for tossing with favorite potato salad ingredients.

Boiled Dressing for Potato Salad

1/2 cup vinegar
1 cup water
1/2 cup sugar
1 egg
2 teaspoons prepared yellow mustard
4 tablespoons all-purpose flour mixed with a
        little water to make a liquid
1/2 teaspoon salt
1/4 cup milk

Use heavy pan or double boiler. Bring to boil the vinegar, water, and sugar. Beat together the egg, prepared mustard, and flour/liquid mixture. Add salt. Stir constantly. Lastly, add 1/4 cup milk until the mixture takes on a creamy texture. Toss onto your favorite potato salad makings—boiled potatoes, chopped celery, chopped onions, hard-boiled eggs, etc. Chill until serving time.

We have Jana to thank for this recipe for delicious Okra Salad. Doesn't it just sound like something straight from the country?

Okra Salad

1 (16-ounce) bag frozen, breaded okra, fried
    (or use fresh okra, cut and breaded)
1 pound bacon, fried and crumbled
1 bunch green onion, chopped
1 tomato, diced

Toss and cover with dressing: 1/4 cup vinegar, 1/4 cup vegetable oil, and 1/4 cup sugar, mixed. Chill until ready to serve.

I've always loved this recipe and thought it represented the essence of a country summer picnic.

Potato-Cucumber Casserole

4-5 potatoes, sliced, boiled, and cooled
1-2 cucumbers, peeled and sliced thin
1 or 2 onions (red or green onions)
1 (8-ounce) carton sour cream
3/4 cup mayonnaise
1/8 teaspoon Worcestershire sauce
1/2 teaspoon celery seed

Mix sour cream, mayonnaise, Worcestershire, and celery seed to make a sauce. In a 13-by-9-by-2-inch dish, layer potatoes, cucumbers, onions, and sauce, ending with sauce. Refrigerate overnight.

I've brought this dish to family Thanksgiving meals. I love the combination of cranberry, orange, and pineapple.

Cranberry-Orange Salad

2 (3-ounce) packages orange-flavored gelatin
1 (1-pound) can whole cranberry sauce
14 ounces (1 3/4 cup) gingerale
1 (8 3/4-ounce) can crushed pineapple

Heat cranberry sauce until gelatin is dissolved and almost boiling. Add undrained pineapple and gingerale. Let set until fizzing stops. Pour into a 5-cup mold. Serves 8-10.

When I married into the Moore family, I immediately loved this wonderful homemade dressing that my husband's mother, Grace Moore, poured over all types of salads. It was a recipe that she learned to make from her mother, Mary Alice

Mauldin. Although she most often served it over fruit, it also appeared many times on her green salad of lettuce, tomatoes, and cucumbers. It makes any ordinary salad taste special.

Grandmother's Salad Dressing

3/4 cup mayonnaise
1/2 cup milk
2 tablespoons sugar

Mix in a canning jar. Put on lid. Chill in refrigerator until mixture thickens. Shake jar well and pour dressing over salad. Chill salad before serving.

Vegetables

*

Another of Jana's big-time contributions has been her Sweet Potato Casserole. The crunchy, sweet topping makes those yams go down easy.

Sweet Potato Casserole

> 3 cups sweet potatoes (about 4 good-sized
>   potatoes or 1 1/2 big cans candied
>   yams)
> 1/2 cup sugar
> 1/2 cup (1 stick) margarine
> 2 eggs, beaten
> 1 teaspoon vanilla extract
> 1/3 cup milk
> 1/3 cup margarine, melted
> 1 cup light brown sugar
> 1/2 cup all-purpose flour
> 1 cup chopped pecans

Boil and mash potatoes. Mix in sugar, margarine, eggs, vanilla, and milk. Put in 13-by-9-by-2-inch baking dish. For topping, melt margarine and mix in remaining ingredients. Sprinkle on top of potato mixture. Bake at 350 degrees for 25 minutes. Serves 10-12.

Lynda's Squash Casserole is always devoured quickly.

Squash Casserole

3 pounds yellow squash
2 tablespoons margarine
3 eggs
3 scant tablespoons sugar
1/2 (12-ounce) can evaporated milk
2 tablespoons salt
1 teaspoon pepper
2 tablespoons flour
1/2 cup chopped onion
grated Cheddar cheese

Cook, drain thoroughly, and mash squash. After mashing add remaining ingredients except cheese. Grease 2-quart casserole and pour in mixture. Bake at 375 degrees for 30 minutes. Top with grated cheese.

Spinach Loaf, introduced by Mable, is an unusual and pretty dish and a good way to sneak spinach past a few reluctant eaters.

Spinach Loaf

1 pound spinach, ground in blender
1 cup bread crumbs
1 small green pepper
1 1/2 teaspoons hot chili powder
1/2 tablespoon salt
1/4 teaspoon freshly ground black pepper
1/2 teaspoon nutmeg
1 tablespoon sugar
2 tablespoons margarine
3 eggs, beaten

Mix together and put in greased mold in pan of water. Cook in slow oven at 300 degrees for 45 minutes.

Another quick-disappearing menu item is Yvonne's Potato Casserole, featured below. It's a great side dish to the Oven-Bag Brisket (page 74) when serving a large group.

Potato Casserole

1 (1- to 2-pound) bag frozen hash brown
     potatoes, thawed
1/2 cup chopped onions
2 (8-ounce) cartons sour cream
10 ounces American cheese, grated
1 (10 3/4-ounce) can cream of chicken soup
1 teaspoon salt
1/2 teaspoon freshly ground black pepper
1/2 cup (1 stick) melted margarine

Topping:
2 cups crushed corn flakes
1/4 cup (1/2 stick) melted margarine

Mix potatoes, onions, sour cream, cheese, soup, salt, pepper, and margarine. Pour into a greased 13-by-9-by-2-inch baking pan. Mix corn flakes with melted margarine. Put on top. Bake at 350 degrees for 45 minutes.Serves 8-10.

Hot Fruit Compote, found on the next page, is a traditional Christmas dish in every sense of the word, because I make it only at Christmas time and because of its rich, deep red color. It's included in the vegetable category since it's served warm and as a side dish, although its contents are canned fruits. It's another of those dishes I acquired from the regular *Houston Chronicle* bring-a-dish meals and then began sharing it at family gatherings. Serve any leftovers with a scoop of vanilla ice cream for a wonderful dessert.

Hot Fruit Compote

1 (15-ounce) can peaches
1 (15 1/4-ounce) can pears
1 (20-ounce) can pineapple chunks
1 (15-ounce) can dark sweet cherries
1 or 2 (11-ounce) cans mandarin oranges
1/2 cup (1 stick) margarine
3 tablespoons cornstarch
1 cup juices from drained fruits, above
1/4 cup brown sugar
1 to 2 teaspoons almond extract

Drain fruits, reserving juices. Cut fruits into chunks. Set aside. In a saucepan melt margarine; combine with cornstarch, juices, and brown sugar until thick. Add almond extract. Combine sauce and fruit and bake in greased casserole at 325 degrees for 45 minutes. Serves 14.

Besides Marcie's famous Broccoli Salad, which appeared on page 78, we also got from Marcie's family this memorable Corn Casserole, which was served during our get-acquainted dinner with her parents in Arizona before she and Matthew married. We quickly integrated it into our family's line.

Corn Casserole

1/2 cup (1 stick) margarine, melted
1 egg
1 (8-ounce) carton sour cream
1 (8 1/2-ounce) box corn bread mix
2 (15-ounce) cans cream-style corn
1 can whole kernel corn

Mix together. Bake at 350 degrees for one hour in a greased 13-by-9-by-2-inch baking dish. Serves 10-12.

Mable's Delicious Corn is probably one of the most enduring dishes in this collection. It's been on the family Christmas dinner table for years and years and is a special favorite of my cousin, Mark.

Delicious Corn

1 large onion, chopped
1 medium green pepper, chopped
2 tablespoons bacon drippings
1/2 cup (1 stick) margarine
1/2 (10-ounce) can tomatoes and green chilies, drained
1 (14 1/2-ounce) can tomatoes, drained
2 (15-ounce) cans cream-style corn (1 yellow, 1 white)
2 (15-ounce) cans whole corn (1 yellow, 1 white)
1 tablespoon sugar

Saute onion and green pepper in bacon drippings and add margarine and tomatoes and bring to a boil. Add corn and sugar. Mix and pour into a 3-quart baking dish and bake at 350 degrees for 30 minutes. Serves 12-14.

Another of Mable's contributions is this delicious Cheesy Lima Casserole, which was a staple of my childhood.

Cheesy Lima Casserole

2 (10-ounce) packages frozen lima beans
1 (10 3/4-ounce) can cream of mushroom soup
grated Cheddar cheese

Cook lima beans according to package directions, until tender. Season with 1 tablespoon margarine. In a greased square casserole dish, alternate layers of lima beans, soup, and cheese, ending with cheese. Bake at 350 degrees for 30 minutes. Serves 4-6.

Whereas some picky eaters may politely decline a vegetable dish here or there, not one participant at a family meal ever bypasses Yvonne's Cinnamon Apples. They are a favorite of diners of all ages.

Cinnamon Apples

4 to 5 large baking apples
1 cup sugar
1/2 cup red hot cinnamon candies

Cook apples in small amount of water until soft. Add cinnamon candies that have been melted in 1/2 cup water in microwave. Add sugar and cook until most of liquid is gone. Red food color can be added, if desired. Serves 8-10.

This Sunshine Carrot dish was served at our family's celebration dinner for Aunt Frances' 95th birthday, a grand occasion, to be sure.

Sunshine Carrots

5 medium carrots, cut into 1-inch chunks
1 tablespoon sugar
1 teaspoon cornstarch
1/4 teaspoon salt
1/4 teaspoon ground ginger
1/4 cup orange juice
2 tablespoons margarine

Cook carrots until tender, drain. In small saucepan combine next four ingredients. Add orange juice; cook, stirring constantly, until mixture thickens. Add margarine. Stir well. Pour over carrots. Toss to coat. Serves 4.

Having our own garden and watching our own vegetables spring up from the earth before our very eyes has been one of our great delights. I always had thought only Aunt Bonnie was capable of bringing forth nature's yield, so when I saw that (with God's help) I was capable of such an act, I was incredulous. Besides beets for Aunt Bonnie's recipe of beet pickles, here's another favorite way that we have used this vegetable.

Ruby-Sauced Beets

5 cups fresh beets—sliced, cooked, and
        drained (or 3 16-ounce cans beets)
4 teaspoons all-purpose flour
2 teaspoons sugar
1/4 teaspoon salt
1 1/3 cups cranberry juice cocktail
1 small orange

In large saucepan, blend cornstarch, sugar, and salt. Stir in cranberry juice cook and stir over medium heat until thick and bubbly. Add drained beets and 1 teaspoon grated orange peel. Simmer uncovered for 10 minutes. Garnish with orange slices. Serves 10-12.

The years that I had the privilege of working alongside revered *Houston Chronicle* Food Editor Ann Criswell and occupying a neighboring cubicle in the *Chronicle* office complex were true learning experiences. I owe so many good recipes to her collection, which she often let her co-workers taste-test before she printed these menu items in her food section. Arriving at work each day was an adventure as those of us who worked around Ann never knew what dish she'd bring for us to sample. We always looked forward to the completion of one of Ann's photo shoots for her section, so we could sample the items photographed. The following recipe for Green Beans Supreme, which I prepared for many family Thanksgiving meals, was one of Ann's best.

Green Beans Supreme

1/2 cup sliced onion
1 tablespoon fresh parsley
4 tablespoons margarine, divided
2 tablespoons all-purpose flour
1 teaspoon salt
1/4 teaspoon freshly ground black pepper
1/2 cup dried bread crumbs
1/2 teaspoon fresh lemon juice
1 (8-ounce) carton sour cream
5 cups cooked green beans, drained
1/2 cups grated Cheddar cheese

Saute onions and parsley in 2 tablespoons margarine until onions and parsley are tender. Add flour, salt, pepper, and lemon juice, stirring. Add sour cream, then drained green beans. Heat but do not boil. Turn into 2-quart greased casserole dish. Top with grated cheese. In a small saucepan melt remaining 2 tablespoons margarine; stir in bread crumbs. Sprinkle crumb topping over beans. Broil at low heat until cheese melts and crumbs brown. Serves 6.

The first Thanksgiving after we had relocated in Texas after more than 12 years of living in the eastern half of the country was a joyful time for us because we could host the family in our own home after years of being away and of missing many family Thanksgivings. I prepared this dish of Vegetables Au Gratin for our first Texas Thanksgiving back home. I borrowed the recipe from Jane Elder, one of the valued acquaintances I made while we lived on the East Coast.

Vegetables Au Gratin

4 cups cooked vegetables (any kind you like)
1/2 cup crushed cornflakes
1 tablespoon melted margarine

Cook vegetables and set aside. Toss together cornflakes and margarine. Set aside for topping.

3 tablespoons margarine
1/3 cup chopped onion
3 tablespoons all-purpose flour
1 teaspoon salt
1/8 teaspoon freshly ground black pepper
1 1/2 cup milk
1 cup grated Cheddar cheese
1 tablespoon dried or fresh snipped parsley

Saute margarine and onion in saucepan over low heat. Stir in flour, salt, and pepper. Cook, stirring until bubbly. Add milk. Cook and stir until smooth. Add grated cheese. Stir until melted. Remove from heat. Add cooked vegetables and parsley. Spread mixture in shallow 1 1/2-quart or 2-quart baking dish that has been sprayed with cooking spray. Sprinkle cornflakes mixture evenly over top. Bake at 350 degrees for 20 minutes or until sauce is heated and bubbly. Let stand 3-5 minutes before serving. Serves 6-8.

Breads

*

Lynda's Pumpkin Bread tastes like a holiday. Besides being good Christmas and Thanksgiving fare, it's also great to serve on family trips. Slice it in bite-sized pieces and take it along to snack on in the car. It's not too sweet and doesn't mess up little hands like cookies do.

Pumpkin Bread

3 eggs
1 1/2 cups sugar
1 1/2 cups fresh-cooked or canned pumpkin
1 cup plus 2 tablespoons vegetable oil
1 1/2 teaspoons vanilla extract
2 1/4 cups all-purpose flour
1 1/2 teaspoons baking soda
1 1/2 teaspoons baking powder
1 1/2 teaspoons salt
1 1/2 teaspoons ground cinnamon
1/4 teaspoon each cloves, ginger, and nut-
      meg
3/4 cup chopped pecans

Beat eggs and sugar together well. Add pumpkin, oil, and vanilla. Mix thoroughly. Sift dry ingredients; add to pumpkin mixture. Add pecans. Bake at 350 degrees for one hour in two well-greased loaf pans.

130

Our family's Corn Bread Dressing has always been just the very best. No cafeteria or restaurant has ever been able to come close to replicating the kind of dressing that's served alongside the turkey on our Thanksgiving Day table. Yvonne shares the secret here.

Corn Bread Dressing

2 large pans corn bread
1 package small hamburger buns
4 eggs (or egg substitute)
broth—enough to make thin mixture
1/2 cup each onion and celery
salt, freshly ground black pepper, sage, poultry seasoning to taste

Crumble corn bread and hamburger buns. Add chopped onions, celery, seasonings, and eggs. Mix well. Add broth to make desired consistency. Spray 13-by-9-by-2-inch baking pan with cooking spray and pour in dressing. Bake at 350 degrees about 45 minutes until dressing is set and slightly browned. Continue to pour a little broth over the dressing several times as it cooks to keep it from drying out. Serves 12-14.

When Louis and I made our six-year foray into Virginia, we discovered some traditional favorite dishes from that part of the country. One of those is the recipe for Ham Biscuits, truly a Virginia staple—for breakfast or with any meal. The recipe that follows has made its way back to Texas with us and now integrates with my East Texas farm-cooking heritage.

Ham Biscuits

3 dozen small biscuits (most people use a
    package of small dinner rolls)
2 sticks margarine at room temperature
1 tablespoon Worcestershire sauce
3 tablespoons prepared yellow mustard
3 teaspoons poppy seed
1 medium chopped onion
3 ounces shredded Swiss cheese
8 ounces chopped ham (most use a
    can of chopped ham)

Split rolls; set aside. Combine all remaining
ingredients. Spread mixture on one side of
rolls; close rolls; wrap in foil, bake at 350
degrees for 10-12 minutes. Ham biscuits can
be frozen for several months and served
later.

Louis' family enjoyed dumplings with everything, so I had
to quickly learn this Fluffy Dumplings recipe after we married.

Fluffy Dumplings

1 cup all-purpose flour
2 teaspoons baking powder
1/2 teaspoon salt
1/2 cup milk
2 tablespoons vegetable oil

Sift flour, baking powder, and salt together
into mixing bowl. Combine milk and oil; add
all at once to dry ingredients, stirring until
moist. Drop from tablespoon atop bubbling
stew. Cover tightly, let mixture return to boiling. Reduce heat; simmer 12-15 minutes.
Makes 10 dumplings.

The advent of the bread machine has made it a snap to have homemade yeast rolls for special dining occasions. These made their debut at Aunt Frances' 95th birthday luncheon.

Basic Dinner Rolls
(for Bread Machine)

3/4 cup plus 3 tablespoons water
3 cups bread flour
2 tablespoons dry milk
3 1/2 tablespoons sugar
1 teaspoon salt
3 tablespoons margarine
2 teaspoons active dry yeast

Add lukewarm water to bread pan. Add bread flour, dry milk, sugar, and salt to pan. Tap pan to settle dry ingredients, then level ingredients, pushing some of the mixture into corners. Place margarine into corners of pan. Make a well in center of dry ingredients; add yeast. Lock pan into bread machine. Program for dough. Start bread machine. When done, remove pan from bread machine. Place dough onto floured surface. Let rest 15 minutes. Spray muffin pan with cooking spray. Roll small pieces of dough into balls. Place 3 balls into greased muffin cup to form a cloverleaf roll. Dough makes enough for 1 1/2 dozen cloverleaf rolls. Brush each roll with softened margarine. Cover and let rise until double in size (about 45 minutes). Bake in 350-degree oven for 15-20 minutes or until golden brown.

These No-Rise Cinnamon Rolls are appealing because no rising process is required. I could quickly churn out a batch of these on Saturday mornings when our children were growing up. When Matthew went off to college, he asked for these when he made return trips home.

No-Rise Cinnamon Rolls

2 (1/4-ounce) packages active dry yeast
1 1/4 cups warm water
margarine
1 teaspoon salt
1 (4 1/2-ounce) package egg custard mix
3 3/4 cups all-purpose flour
1/2 cup brown sugar
1/2 teaspoon ground cinnamon
1/4 cup chopped pecans

Dissolve yeast in warm water. Add 1/4 cup melted margarine, salt, and custard mix. Stir well. Add flour gradually. Turn out onto well-floured board and knead about 5 times, until no longer sticky. Preheat oven to 375 degrees, about 10 minutes. Roll dough out 1/4-inch thick in a 18x10 inch rectangle. Melt 3 table-spoons margarine and spread evenly over dough. Mix sugar, cinnamon, and pecans and distribute over dough evenly. Roll up like a jelly roll from the long side. Cut into 1-inch thick slices and place on a cookie sheet, cut side down. Bake at 375 degrees for 10-15 minutes. Frost with icing. Makes 18.

Icing:
2 cups less 1 tablespoon powdered sugar, sifted
2 tablespoons margarine
1 1/2 teaspoons vanilla extract
1 to 2 tablespoons warm water

The following three quick-bread recipes—Pear Bread on this page and Pineapple Macadamia Nut Bread and Banana Honey Muffins on the next—are those that I have made and given as Christmas gifts for the family.

Pear Bread

1 cup vegetable oil
2 cups granulated sugar
3 eggs
2 1/2 cups peeled and chopped fresh pears
1 cup chopped pecans
2 teaspoons vanilla extract
3 cups all-purpose flour
1 teaspoon baking soda
1/2 teaspoon salt
1 teaspoon ground cinnamon
1/2 teaspoon ground nutmeg

Preheat oven to 350 degrees. Combine oil, sugar, and eggs. Stir in pears, pecans, and vanilla. In another bowl, combine remaining ingredients. Stir dry ingredients into the pear mixture. Pour the batter into two greased loaf pans. Bake loaves for one hour or until a toothpick comes out clean. This bread can also be baked in 4 greased pint canning jars. Place jars on an ungreased baking sheet. Pour in bread dough. Bake jars 40 minutes or until a toothpick comes out clean. Cool bread in jars completely.

Pineapple Macadamia Nut Bread

3/4 cup chopped Macadamia nuts
1 cup pineapple tidbits, drained
1 1/2 teaspoon soda
1/2 teaspoon salt
3 tablespoons softened shortening
1 (8 1/4-ounce) can crushed, undrained
    pineapple
2 eggs
1 teaspoon vanilla extract
1 cup sugar
2 cups all-purpose flour

Grease 9x5 loaf pan. Using fork, mix nuts,
drained pineapple, soda, and salt. Add shortening and hot crushed pineapple. Beat eggs,
vanilla, and sugar. Stir in flour. Add pineapple mixture. Stir until just well blended. Bake
at 350 degrees for one hour.

Banana Honey Muffins

3/4 cup whole-wheat flour
3/4 cup all-purpose flour
2 teaspoons baking powder
1/2 teaspoon salt
3/4 cup oatmeal, uncooked
1/4 cup honey
1 egg
3/4 cup milk
1/3 cup mashed bananas
1/4 cup vegetable oil

Combine all dry ingredients in one bowl and
all liquid ingredients in another. Stir until just
evenly moist. Spoon into greased muffin
cups. Bake at 400 degrees for 15 minutes.

This recipe for Jalapeno Corn Bread was a hit with Oven-Bag Brisket at Aunt Frances' 95th birthday luncheon. It also goes great with soups and vegetables. The consistency is between corn bread and spoon bread, but it is firm enough to cut into squares or wedges.

Jalapeno Corn Bread

> 2 cups cream-style corn
> 2 cups corn bread mix
> 2/3 cup vegetable oil
> 4 eggs, beaten
> 2 (8-ounce) cartons sour cream
> 1 1/2-2 cups grated Cheddar cheese (can
>   use part reduced-fat)
> 1 cup chopped onion
> 1 (4-ounces) can jalapenos or green chilies,
>   drained, seeded, and chopped

> Preheat oven to 350 degrees. Grease a 13-by-9-by-2-inch pan. In large bowl combine corn, corn bread mix, oil, eggs, sour cream, cheese, onion, and jalapenos. Mix well. Pour batter into prepared pan and bake for about 1 hour. Recipe can be halved easily. Serves 12-15.

My sister-in-law, Mary Emerson, is one of the best pastry cooks around. Her basic bread dough makes some terrific dinner rolls. Her recipe on the next page also includes variations for whole-wheat and oatmeal bread.

Basic Bread Dough

6-7 cups all-purpose flour
1/4 cup sugar
1 tablespoon salt
2 (1/4-ounce) packages active dry yeast
2 1/4 cups milk
1/4 cup vegetable oil
1 egg

Combine 2 cups of the flour, along with sugar, salt, and yeast. Heat milk and oil in saucepan over low heat until warm (120-130 degrees). Add egg and warm liquid to flour mixture. Beat thoroughly. Stir in another 4-5 cups flour to form a soft dough. Knead on floured surface until smooth, about 1 minute. Place dough in greased bowl. Cover and let rise in warm place until doubled in size, 45-60 minutes. Punch down dough. Place in two greased 9x5 loaf pans. Cover and let rise in warm place until light for 30-45 minutes. Bake 350 degrees for 40-45 minutes.

Dinner rolls: After rising once, shape dough into rolls of desired shape. Place on greased cookie sheet. Brush with a mixture of 1 beaten egg and 1 tablespoon milk. Let rise 30-45 minutes. Bake at 400 degrees for 12-15 minutes.
Whole-wheat bread: Substitute 3 cups whole-wheat flour for first 3 cups all-purpose flour.
Oatmeal bread: Add 1 1/2 cups quick oats to dry flour-yeast mixture.

Main Dish Recipes

*

No point in beating around the bush. I'll go right to the heart of this category and get the secret out on the table. It's the recipe for how the families of the Red-Haired Miller Girls prepare the holiday turkey. When I first saw my mother do this, years ago before turkey-cooking became my responsibility, I thought she was making a big mistake. Whoever heard of baking a sizeable, 12-pound bird for only an hour? Surely she had misread a recipe somewhere. Yet her turkeys always turned out great, following the instructions below. Then one day it came my turn to prepare the Thanksgiving meal. I tried the following method, and it worked perfectly. The turkey comes out gorgeously brown and moist, no basting required. With this recipe, the cook can always get a good night's sleep before the big day and can rest confidently that the perfect bird will be served.

One-Hour Turkey

Rinse thawed turkey. Stuff turkey with chopped apples, celery, and onions. Place in roasting pan with lid. Add 2 cups water and cover. Place in an oven that has been preheated to 500 degrees. Cook for 1 hour. Turn off burner and leave in oven overnight. Do NOT open oven or remove cover until morning. Carve and serve.

To go with the turkey, here's Mable's recipe for Giblet Gravy. Like the turkey, this gravy is fool-proof.

Giblet Gravy

Place heart, gizzard, and neck in covered pan with four cups water, 1 sliced onion, and 1 teaspoon pepper. Cook until tender, about 2 hours and 15 minutes. Before cooking time has elapsed, add liver. Drain giblets and reserve stock. Chop giblets. Add 6 table-spoons turkey fat and 6 tablespoons all-purpose flour, stirring to make smooth mixture. Add four cups of broth. Boil 5 minutes. Add more salt and pepper to taste. Stir in chopped giblets and a hard-boiled egg, chopped.

This Chicken Spaghetti recipe of Frances' is memorable.

Chicken Spaghetti

1 (14 1/2-ounce) can whole tomatoes
1 (10 3/4-ounce) can cream of mushroom soup
1 fryer, boiled and boned
1 (8-ounce) box spaghetti
1/2 cup each chopped small onion and small green pepper
1 cup chopped celery
1 (2-ounce) jar pimiento
Worcestershire sauce, salt, and pepper to taste

Dice chicken and add it to cooked spaghetti. Saute onion and pepper in 1 tablespoon margarine. Add other ingredients, add broth, and cook liquid cooks down some. Pour into 13-by-9-by-2-inch greased baking dish. Top with cheese and bake in 350-degree oven until cheese melts.

Mable's Chicken and Wild Rice Casserole was first intro-duced at a bridal shower but quickly became a regular at family gatherings.

Chicken and Wild Rice Casserole

1 cup wild rice
1/2 cup chopped onion
1/2 cup (1 stick) margarine
1/4 cup all-purpose flour
1 (6-ounce) can sliced mushrooms
1 1/2 cups chicken broth
1 1/2 cups light cream
3 cups diced, cooked chicken
1/4 cup diced pimiento
2 tablespoons fresh parsley
1 1/2 teaspoons salt
1/4 teaspoon freshly ground black pepper
1/2 cup slivered almonds

Prepare 1 cup wild rice according to package directions. Cook onion in margarine until ten-der. Remove from heat. Stir in flour. Drain mushrooms, reserving liquid. Add broth to make 1 1/2 cups. Add cream; cook and stir until mixture thickens. Add rest of ingredi-ents. Pour into 2-quart, greased casserole dish. Sprinkle with slivered almonds. Bake at 350 degrees for 25-30 minutes. Serves 6-8.

Eleene shares the recipe on the next page for Sausage and Rice Casserole. She obtained it from her in-law family, the Choates. She credits Doris Choate, wife of Joe's brother Clyde, with this contribution. Sausage and Rice Casserole tastes as good on the second and third days as a leftover as it does on the first, fresh from the oven.

Sausage and Rice Casserole

1 pound sausage (mild)
1/4 cup chopped green peppers
1/2 cup chopped celery
1 medium onion, chopped
1 package chicken soup (tested with Lipton ®)
1 cup minute rice
1 (2-ounce) can chopped mushrooms

Brown sausage, pepper, celery, and onion.
Add soup, mushrooms, and four cups of
water. Bring to a boil. Pour over rice and cook
in crock pot for 1 hour on high or in oven at
350 degrees for 1 hour. Serves 6-8.

A meal of Mable's Salmon Croquettes, along with fluffy
mashed potatoes and green peas, was always waiting for our
family of four when Louis and I and the kids came in from a
long drive from wherever we were living and arrived for a
visit, especially for Christmas.

Salmon Croquettes

1 (14 3/4-ounce) can salmon
1 egg
6-8 saltine crackers
dash of salt and freshly ground black pepper
1 medium onion, chopped
vegetable oil

Drain salmon. Remove bones and dark pieces
from salmon and break up pieces. Add beaten
egg and crackers, a few at a time. Mix by hand
until mixture can be made into a patty. Avoid
making too dry. Fry in a skillet in a small
amount of oil. Makes 6-8 croquettes.

One of the first main dishes I ever learned to make in high-school home-economics class was this Meat Loaf. In our house, it has otherwise been known as "Meat Loft" because my kids spotted a spelling error I made long ago on an old recipe card. Although they've teased me about the error in the title, they are never shy about consuming this main dish.

Meat Loaf

1 pound ground beef
1/2 medium onion, chopped
1/2 cup milk
1/2 cup ketchup
1 egg, beaten
1 1/2 slices day-old bread
1 teaspoon salt
1/2 teaspoon freshly ground black pepper
1/4 cup ketchup

Combine ingredients. Spray a loaf pan with non-stick spray. Pour mixture into pan, forming a loaf. Pour 1/4 cup ketchup over the mixture and spread to cover loaf. Bake at 350 degrees for 1 hour. Serves 6.

Another dish to which our kids give high marks is Baked Enchilada Casserole. It's been served weekly during most of our 33-year marriage. I got the recipe when I visited Carma McCollum, who was then a young bride and who later was matron of honor in our wedding. Carma said this was one of the first recipes she cooked when she married her husband, Mike, and that it was great on a student budget. Since Louis and I started married life as he attended seminary, I figured this was one that would come in handy. It did then and has for all these years later. It's great served with Jalapeno Corn Bread (page 136.)

Baked Enchilada Casserole

1 dozen flour tortillas
1 medium onion, chopped
1 (10 3/4-ounce) can cream of chicken soup
1 (10 3/4-ounce) can cream of mushroom soup
1/2 (8-ounce) jar taco sauce
1 pound ground beef
1/2 pound grated Cheddar cheese
1/2 cup milk

In a skillet, brown meat and onion. Add
soups, taco sauce, and milk. Prepare a 2-quart
casserole dish with cooking spray. Tear flour
tortillas into pieces. Line bottom of casserole
dish. Pour onto tortillas a layer of meat mixture, followed by a layer of cheese. Continue
alternating layers, ending with cheese on top
Bake at 350 degrees for 30 minutes. Serves 6.

Eleene says that Mark's family considered this dish a regular when he was growing up. It's simple and tasty.

Ground Meat and Rice Casserole

1/2 cup chopped onion
1/2 cup chopped bell pepper
1 (10-ounce) can tomatoes with green chilies
1 teaspoon chili powder
1 cup uncooked rice
salt and freshly ground pepper to taste

Brown onion and bell pepper in skillet with 2
tablespoons margarine. Add 1 pound ground
meat. Cook until meat is done. Add tomatoes,
chili powder, uncooked rice, salt, and pepper.
Pour into prepared baking dish and cook in
oven at 350 degrees for about 45 minutes.
Serves 6-8.

The way our kids go after this casserole, you'd never believe it contains the dreaded "S"-word—spinach. My sister-in-law, Debbie Moore, let me have her Spinach Lasagna recipe so I could incorporate it among our family favorites.

Spinach Lasagna

1 bunch spinach, rinsed and chopped finely
2 eggs
1 (8-ounce) package Cheddar cheese
1 (8-ounce) package Monterrey Jack cheese
1 (14-ounce) container small-curd cottage
    cheese
1 (1-pound, 10 1/2-ounce) jar spaghetti sauce
1 (14 1/2-ounce) can stewed tomatoes
l (16-ounce) box lasagna noodles

Cook noodles according to package directions. While they cook, combine spinach, eggs, Cheddar cheese, Monterey Jack cheese, cottage cheese, spaghetti sauce, and stewed tomatoes. Put small amount of sauce on bottom of a 13-by-9-by-2-inch greased dish. Drain lasagna noodles. Stretch them out, putting sauce on top of noodles. Roll up noodles. Repeat, lining up rolled noodles in rows until the dish is filled up. Save a little extra sauce to spread on top. Sprinkle Parmesan cheese on top of all. Bake at 350 degrees for 30 minutes. Serves 8-10.

When we've lived in parts of the country where people genuinely asked the question, "What is a grit?", we've taken it upon ourselves to educate these deprived ones through this Baked Cheese Garlic Grits casserole that follows. Although some cooks serve it as a breakfast casserole, around our house it's a main-course dish served regularly.

Baked Cheese Garlic Grits

3 cups water
3/4 cup quick grits
1/2 teaspoon salt
1 cup shredded Cheddar cheese
2 tablespoons margarine
1 egg, beaten
1/8 teaspoon garlic powder
dash red pepper sauce

Grease 1 1/2-quart casserole. Prepare grits according to package directions. Stir in remaining ingredients. Continue cooking over low heat until cheese is melted. Pour into prepared casserole. Bake at 350 degrees for 30 minutes. Serves 4-6.

In the Equal-Time Department, I'd be remiss in leaving out Louis's favorite dish to cook (and believe me, he gets the chance to do so often.) Louis learned to make this Easy Pot Roast by watching his father, Louis Sr., do so.

Easy Pot Roast

Wash a 5-7 pound roast. Put 1 tablespoon vegetable oil in a Dutch oven. In oil, sear the roast on both sides. On each side sprinkle 1/2 teaspoon salt and 1/4 teaspoon pepper. Once meat is seared, add 1 8-ounce glass of hot water, leaving roast top exposed. Add extra water if necessary. Add 1 sliced onion on top of meat. Simmer roast for 1 1/2 -2 hours. While roast cooks, peel 1 dozen potatoes and 2 dozen carrots. When roast appears done, place potatoes and carrots in juice around roast. Add 1 teaspoon salt and 1/2 teaspoon pepper to season vegetables. Let simmer another hour until carrots and potatoes are soft. Juice from pan can be used as gravy.

Mark and Eleene's Marleene, who once helped us keep
our priorities straight with her "Happy Birthday, Jesus" cake,
grew up to be a fine young woman whose priorities about
faith and family are still in order. For her apartment-mates at
college, Marleene made a big hit with this Tortilla Soup.

Tortilla Soup

1 family-size (26-ounce) can chicken and
   rice soup
1 (15-ounce) can ranch-style beans
1 (10-ounce) can tomatoes and green chilies
1 (15-ounce) can cream-style corn
1 (4 1/2-ounce) can chicken

Heat all of the above ingredients together.
Serve with grated cheese on top and with tortilla chips.

Desserts

*

Now, for the real reason this cookbook exists—to preserve all those delectable dessert recipes that we have delighted in over the years. One of these treasures is Mattie's Pecan Pie recipe, just as she prepared it for the Three Red-Haired Miller Girls.

Pecan Pie

3 whole eggs
2 tablespoons melted margarine
2 tablespoons all-purpose flour
1/4 teaspoon vanilla extract
1/8 teaspoon salt
1/2 cup sugar
1 1/2 cups dark corn syrup
1 1/2 cups broken pecan halves
1 unbaked 9-inch pie shell

Beat eggs; blend in melted margarine, flour, vanilla, salt, sugar, and syrup. Sprinkle pecans over the bottom of pie shell. Gently pour syrup mixture over pecans. Bake in hot oven 425 degrees for 10 minutes. Reduce heat to 325 degrees and bake for about 40 minutes.

I love to make this Chocolate Chess Pie for family gatherings and church covered-dish meals, but I can't set my sights on having any leftovers to bring home. It disappears quickly!

Chocolate Chess Pie

1 cup sugar
3 tablespoons cornmeal
3 tablespoons unsweetened cocoa powder
3 eggs, well beaten
1/2 cup (1 stick) margarine, melted
1/2 cup light corn syrup
1 teaspoon vanilla extract
1 unbaked, 9-inch pie shell

Combine and sift sugar, cornmeal, and cocoa; add eggs, margarine, syrup, and vanilla. Pour in pie shell. Bake at 350 degrees for 45 minutes.

Mable carted this Pineapple Pie to Cooper with her on many trips because she knew it was my Uncle Bill's favorite.

Pineapple Pie

1 1/2 cups sugar
1/2 cup all-purpose flour
3 egg yolks (reserve whites)
3 cups milk
pinch of salt
1 tablespoon margarine
1 teaspoon vanilla extract
1 (8-ounce) can crushed pineapple
1 ready-cooked 9-inch pie shell

Mix first five ingredients well and cook until thick. Add margarine, vanilla, and pineapple. Pour into ready-cooked pie shell. (See next page for meringue and crust recipes.)

Meringue for Pineapple Pie

3 egg whites (brought to room temperature)
1/4 teaspoon cream of tartar
1 teaspoon vanilla extract
3 scant tablespoons sugar

Beat until stiff enough to stand in peaks. Cook
in oven until meringue is golden brown.

Katie began making this Easy Pie Crust during one of her
high-school summers as part of "Project Edu-Kate", a fun
time in which we worked together for her to learn some life
skills such as cooking, sewing, and installing plumbing fix-
tures. This recipe turns out a perfect pie crust always. Did
Katie really wow everyone when she produced her first pie, a
double crust apple with a lattice top! It wasn't just beginner's
luck; the easy crust recipe did the trick.

Easy Pie Crust

2 cups all-purpose flour
1 teaspoon salt
2/3 cup vegetable oil
4 tablespoons water

Mix together the flour and salt. Stir the oil in
with a fork. Sprinkle the water over the mixture
and stir with fork until everything is well
blended and no longer sticky. Mix well together
and roll out between two sheets of waxed
paper. Dough makes enough for two crusts, so
divide ball of dough in two and roll out one
crust at time. Peel off paper and fit in pie pan.
Bake at 450 degrees for single crust and at 425
for double crust. Bake until lightly browned.

Louis gets the gold medal in the baking department for coming up with this Pumpkin Cobbler recipe. One year our garden produced so many pumpkins we didn't know what to do with them all, so we found some new and creative ways, such as this one, to use pumpkin.

Pumpkin Cobbler

1 (18 1/4-ounce) package yellow cake mix
3/4 cup (1 1/2 sticks) margarine
3 eggs
3 cups fresh cooked or canned pumpkin
2/3 cup milk
1 3/4 cups sugar
2 1/4 cups brown sugar
2 teaspoons ground cinnamon
1 teaspoon ground nutmeg

Grease bottom only of a 13-by-9-by-2-inch baking pan. Preheat oven to 350 degrees. To make crust, reserve 1 cup cake mix for topping, then combine the rest of the cake mix with 1/2 cup melted margarine and 1 egg. Stir, then press into pan. To make filling, combine pumpkin, 2 eggs, 2/3 cup milk, 1 1/2 cups sugar, brown sugar, 1 teaspoon nutmeg, and 1 teaspoon cinnamon. To make topping, combine 1 cup cake mix, 1/4 cup sugar, 1 teaspoon cinnamon and 1/4 cup margarine, unmelted. Sprinkle over filling. Bake 1 hour. Serve with whipped topping or ice cream.

Eleene furnished us with this Jam Cake recipe on the next page. She says Bonnie made this cake during one of Eleene's first years in the family. "I remember standing in the kitchen at the farm and hearing her say this was one of Granny's (Mattie's) recipes," Eleene wrote on a note that came with her recipe card.

Jam Cake

2 cups sugar
1 cup (2 sticks) margarine
3 eggs, beaten
1 cup buttermilk
1 cup jam (blackberry is good)
1 cup flaked coconut
1 cup raisins
1 1/2 cup pecans
3 cups all-purpose flour
1 teaspoon soda

Cream margarine and sugar. Add eggs, then add remaining ingredients. Grease and flour four round cake pans. Bake at 300 degrees for 25 to 30 minutes.

Icing for Jam Cake:
1 1/2 cups milk
1 1/2 cups pecans
1 cup flaked coconut
1/2 cup jam
1 cup raisins

Cook the milk as you would for caramel icing. Then add pecans, coconut, jam, and raisins. Frost cake.

When I think about the phrase, "Nothin' says lovin' like somethin from the oven," this Chocolate Dream Cake on the next page comes to mind, since I believe Aunt Bonnie made special efforts to fix it when a little brown-haired girl came to dine. The Dream Frosting that goes with it is truly a dream come true.

Chocolate Dream Cake

2 cups all-purpose flour
2 cups sugar
1/2 cup (1 stick) margarine
1 cup solid all-vegetable shortening
1 cup water
1/4 cup unsweetened cocoa powder
1/2 cup buttermilk
2 eggs, slightly beaten
1 teaspoon soda
1 teaspoon vanilla extract
1 teaspoon ground cinnamon (optional)

Sift flour and sugar into mixing bowl; blend well. Bring to rapid boil in saucepan the margarine, shortening, water, and cocoa. Pour over flour-sugar mixture and mix well. Pour into greased, lightly floured 13-by-9-by-2-inch baking pan and bake at 400 degrees for 35-40 minutes or until it tests done. Let cool for 10-15 minutes while you prepare frosting.

Dream Frosting

1/2 cup (1 stick) margarine
3 1/2 tablespoons unsweetened cocoa powder
1 teaspoon vanilla extract
2/3 cup chopped pecans
1 (1-pound) box powdered sugar, sifted
1/3 cup milk

Combine margarine, cocoa, and milk in saucepan; heat slowly and bring to a boil. Add remaining ingredients; beat well and spread over cake while it is still warm.

A different twist on a chocolate cake is Mable's Anniversary Pound Cake. It's the one that her grandchildren peek under cake-plate covers to find when they come for a visit.

Anniversary Pound Cake

1 cup (2 sticks) margarine
1 cup solid all-vegetable shortening
3 cups sugar
5 eggs
3 cups all-purpose flour
1/2 teaspoon salt
1/2 teaspoon baking powder
5 tablespoons unsweetened cocoa powder
1 cup milk
1 tablespoon vanilla extract

Grease and flour tube or bundt pan. Cream margarine, shortening, and sugar. Add eggs, one at a time. Sift flour, salt, baking powder, and cocoa. Add to creamed mixture alternately with milk and vanilla. Beat after each addition. Bake at 325 degrees for one hour.

Icing:
1 (1-pound) box powdered sugar
1/2 cup (1 stick) margarine, melted
1 egg white
1 teaspoon lemon flavoring
1 (1-ounce) squares unsweetened chocolate, melted
1 cup chopped pecans
1 teaspoon vanilla extract

Beat all ingredients until smooth. Add a little water, if necessary. Frost cooled cake.

156

Two more yummy and sinfully rich chocolate cakes appear next—Eleene's Mississippi Mud Cake and Mable's revered German Chocolate Cake recipes.

Mississippi Mud Cake

1 cup (2 sticks) margarine
1/2 cup unsweetened cocoa powder
4 eggs
2 cups sugar
1 1/2 cups all-purpose flour
1 cup chopped pecans
1 cup coconut
1 (7-ounce) jar marshmallow creme

Mix margarine and cocoa together. Using large bowl, cream sugar, flour, and eggs. Add cocoa mixture. Add pecans and coconut. Pour into greased 13-by-9-by-2-inch baking pan and bake at 350 degrees. After 30 minutes, remove from oven and, while hot, spread 1/2 jar marshmallow creme on top. While cake bakes, prepare icing.

Icing:
1/2 cup (1 stick) margarine
1 (1-pound) box powdered sugar
1/2 cup evaporated milk
1/2 cup unsweetened cocoa powder
1 teaspoon vanilla extract
1 cup chopped pecans

Mix cocoa with melted sugar. Add remaining ingredients. Mix well and pour on top of cake and marshmallow creme. Swirl for "mud" effect.

German Chocolate Cake

1 cup solid all-vegetable shortening
2 cups sugar
3/4 cup buttermilk
4 eggs, separated
2 1/2 cups all-purpose flour
1/2 teaspoon salt
1 teaspoon soda
1/4 cup buttermilk
1 (4-ounce) package German Chocolate

Cream shortening and sugar; add egg yolks. Add flour and salt alternately, with 3/4 cup buttermilk. Add 1/4 cup buttermilk mixed with soda. Melt 1 package German Chocolate in 1/2 cup boiling water. Fold in egg whites. Bake in three pans at 350 degrees for 35 minutes, or until done. Start testing at about 25 minutes to see if cake springs back in center. Time isn't as important as is test for doneness.

Frosting:
6 egg yolks
1 cup chopped pecans
1/4 cup (1/2 stick) margarine
1 (14-ounce) can sweetened condensed milk
2 cups sugar
1 cup flaked coconut
1 teaspoon vanilla extract

Mix and cook to a custard stage. Cool and spread on cooled layers of cake.

I have one cake that I always make as fall arrives. This tasty Sour Cream Apple Cake is a wonderful way to welcome the season.

Sour Cream Apple Cake

2 cups all-purpose flour
2 cups brown sugar
1/2 cup (1 stick) margarine
1 cup chopped pecans
1 or 2 teaspoons ground cinnamon
1 teaspoon soda
1/2 teaspoon salt
1 (8-ounce) carton sour cream
1 teaspoon vanilla extract
1 egg
2 cups chopped apples

Mix first three ingredients until crumbly and stir in pecans. Press 2 3/4 cups of this mixture into 13-by-9-by-2-inch pan. To remaining mixture, add the rest of the ingredients and blend well. Bake at 350 degrees for 25-35 minutes. Serve with vanilla ice cream or whipped topping.

This Applesauce Cake recipe is a lasting reminder of Aunt Mabel, the youngest of Grandma Harris' children and for whom Mable, the Red-Haired Miller Girl, was named. The cooking instructions make it a "must read." Aunt Mabel was a special treasure to be around since she long outlived all of her siblings and always seemed a little reminder of Mattie still left on this earth, especially to Bonnie, Frances, and Mable, who missed their mother. Following Aunt Mabel's is Bonnie's version of Applesauce Cake.

Applesauce Cake

1 cup mincemeat, cut fine

3 eggs

1 cup dates, chopped

1 cup pecans, chopped

1 1/2 cups apples (cut fine and cook in small
     amount of water, then drain)

1/2 cup (1 stick) margarine

2 cups all-purpose flour

1 cup sugar

1/2 teaspoon salt

1 teaspoon ground cinnamon

2 teaspoon ground allspice

1 (6-ounce jar) bottle maraschino cherries

2 teaspoon soda

1 teaspoon vanilla extract

Mix all ingredients. Mix in apples only after
they cool. Pour into greased 13-by-9-by-2-inch
baking pan. Bake in very slow oven with pan
of water under cake. (Flame in oven should be
beads instead of flame.) Bake 1 1/2 hour until
done. It may take longer, but don't cook too
fast.

Bonnie's Applesauce Cake that follows is a layer cake and
features an icing.

Applesauce Cake

2 cups sugar
3/4 cup solid all-vegetable shortening
2 well-beaten eggs
2 cups all-purpose flour
2 teaspoons soda
2 teaspoons ground cinnamon
1 teaspoon cloves
1 teaspoon ground allspice
1 teaspoon salt
2 cups applesauce
1/2 cup warm water
1 cup raisins
1 cup chopped pecans
1 teaspoon vanilla extract

Cream sugar and shortening. Add well-beaten
eggs. Sift together flour, soda, cinnamon,
cloves, allspice, and salt. Add to creamed mixture the applesauce and warm water. Add the
flour mixture, raisins, pecans, and vanilla. Bake
in layers at 350 degrees until cake springs back
in center.

Icing:
3 cups sugar
1 cup milk
1/2 cup (1 stick) margarine
1 cup raisins
1 cup chopped pecans
1 teaspoon vanilla extract
pinch of salt

Cook sugar and milk to soft ball stage. Add
margarine, raisins, pecans, vanilla, and salt.
Mix well. Frost cooled cake.

It never seemed like Christmas until we saw Bonnie's Orange Slice Cake appear on the dessert table. Long after newer recipes replaced it in popularity, family members kept making it for Christmas, just for old times' sake. It makes an excellent fruit-cake alternative.

Orange Slice Cake

2 cups sugar
1 cup (2 sticks) margarine
4 eggs
4 cups all-purpose flour
pinch of salt
1 1/3 cups buttermilk
1 teaspoon soda
3 teaspoons grated orange rind
1 package dates
1 (16-ounce) package orange slice candy, chopped
1 cup chopped pecans
1 teaspoon vanilla extract

Cream margarine and sugar. Add eggs and beat well. Add flour, salt, and buttermilk alternately. Roll dates, pecans, and orange slices in part of flour. Add to dough, Pour into a greased and floured tube cake pan. Bake at 350 degrees for 1 hour and 40 minutes.

Icing:
1 1/2 cups orange juice
2 tablespoons grated orange rind
2 1/4 cups sugar

Boil this about 7 to 10 minutes. Pour icing over cake while cake is hot. Leave cake in pan overnight so icing can all soak into the cake.

162

This cake brought many chuckles as we have imagined Yvonne and Joe furtively purchasing some of the ingredients that were not normal items on their Baptist pantry shelf.

Black Russian Cake

1 (18 1/4-ounce) box yellow cake mix
1 (4 1/2-ounce) box instant pudding mix
1 cup vegetable oil
4 eggs
3/4 cup water
1/4 cup vodka
1/4 cup Kahlua

Combine all ingredients and beat until smooth. Pour into greased and floured bundt pan. Bake at 350 degrees for about one hour. Cool in pan 30 minutes before removing.

Chocolate glaze:
2 tablespoons unsweetened cocoa powder
1 tablespoon vegetable oil
1 tablespoon plus 2 teaspoons water
1 tablespoon corn syrup
1 cup powdered sugar, sifted

Mix over low heat until smooth. Remove from heat and stir in powdered sugar. Drizzle glaze over cake.

Many may remember the popularity of the Sock-It-to-Me Cake in the 1970s. It suddenly became "the" recipe for friends to borrow. Frances' Sock-It-to-Me Cake is wonderful because she tops it with a delicious glaze.

Sock-It-to-Me Cake

1 (18 1/4-ounce) box butter recipe cake mix
1 (8-ounce) carton sour cream
1/2 cup vegetable oil
1/4 cup sugar
1/4 cup water
4 eggs

Blend oil, sugar, water, and eggs. Fold in sour cream. Beat 2 minutes. Add cake mix.

Filling:
1 cup chopped pecans
1/4 cup brown sugar
2 teaspoons ground cinnamon

Pour 2/3 of the batter into greased, floured bundt cake pan. Sprinkle filling over this. Add rest of the batter. Bake at 350-375 degrees for 45-55 minutes.

Glaze:
2 cups powdered sugar, sifted
dash salt
1 teaspoon vanilla extract
light cream
dash salt
1 teaspoon vanilla extract

Add light cream to sifted powdered sugar until it reaches the consistency of glaze (thinner than regular frosting.) Add salt and vanilla. Drizzle over cake.

Mable's Fresh Apple Cake tastes like a crisp, fall day and is wonderful served slightly warm with whipped topping on top. The addition of strawberry and apricot preserves makes it especially moist.

Fresh Apple Cake

4 apples, cut in thin slices
2 cups sugar
1 cup vegetable oil
3 cups all-purpose flour
2 eggs
1 cup chopped pecans
1/2 cup strawberry preserves
1/2 cup apricot preserves
2 teaspoons soda
2 teaspoons vanilla extract
1/2 teaspoon salt
1 teaspoon ground cinnamon
1/2 teaspoon ground allspice
1/4 teaspoon ground nutmeg

Slice apples and add sugar and let stand 20 minutes. Add oil and eggs. Then add all other ingredients. Bake at 300 degrees for 1 1/2 hours in a greased and floured bundt or tube pan.

Mable has baked more loaves of this Cranberry Pudding Cake (recipe on the next page) than anyone can count. Besides bringing them to the family Christmas meal, she annually takes these along on her Christmas visit to shut-ins. These loaves, wrapped in foil, freeze extremely well. Slices of this cake are wonderful served warm with a little margarine spread on them.

Cranberry Pudding Cake

1 (18 1/4-ounce) package yellow cake mix
1 (1-ounce) package lemon instant pudding
4 eggs
1/4 cup vegetable oil
1 (8-ounce) carton sour cream
1 1/2 cups slivered almonds
1 (16-ounce) can jellied cranberry sauce

Mix first six ingredients with spoon. Beat 4 minutes with mixer at medium speed. Cut cranberry sauce into cubes and fold into mixture. Bake in two greased and floured loaf pans at 350 degrees for 55 minutes.

Bonnie also made this derivation of her famous Dream Chocolate Cake. This one has mayonnaise added to the mixture.

Mayonnaise Devil's Food Cake

1 cup mayonnaise
1 cup hot water
1 teaspoon soda
1 teaspoon vanilla extract
1 1/2 cups sugar
2 cups all-purpose flour
2/3 cup unsweetened cocoa powder
1 teaspoon baking powder

Cream mayonnaise, sugar, and cocoa. Dissolve soda in hot water and add alternately with flour. Bake in layers at 350 degrees until cake springs back to touch. Frost with chocolate frosting.

The following Coca-Cola® Cake of Bonnie's has always been a winner. The younger set was surprised to realize that cola could be used in other ways besides to guzzle down.

Coca-Cola® Cake

2 cups sugar
2 cups all-purpose flour
2 eggs
1/2 cup buttermilk
1 teaspoon soda

Combine this first mixture. Set aside.

3 tablespoons unsweetened cocoa powder
1 cup Coca-Cola®
1 cup (2 sticks) margarine
1/2 teaspoon salt
1 1/2 cups marshmallows

Boil cocoa, Coca-Cola® , margarine, and salt. When this mixture comes to a boil, pour in first mixture. Then add marshmallows. Bake at 350 degrees for 40 minutes.

Icing:
3 tablespoons unsweetened cocoa powder
1/2 cup (1 stick) margarine
6 tablespoons Coca-Cola®
1 (1-pound) box powdered sugar

Boil cocoa, margarine, and Coca-Cola®. Let cool. Stir in box of powdered sugar. When cake is cool, frost.

Frances' Mandarin Orange Cake is a fluffy delight. Everyone is always thrilled when we hear she's bringing this to a family meal.

Mandarin Orange Cake

1 (18 1/4-ounce) box yellow cake mix
1 cup butter-flavored vegetable oil
4 eggs
1 (11-ounce) can mandarin oranges, undrained

Mix well the cake mix, oil, eggs, and undrained oranges. Bake in four round cake pans. Bake at 350 degrees for 15 minutes. Cool before icing.

Icing:
1 (20-ounce) can crushed pineapple
1 (3 1/2-ounce) can flaked coconut
1 (5 1/4-ounce) package vanilla instant pudding
1 (16-ounce) container whipped topping

Mix pineapple, coconut, and pudding. Fold in whipped topping. Put between layers and on top. Keep well refrigerated.

These next four Christmas recipes are from Bonnie's collection.

Chocolate Candy

4 1/2 cups sugar
1/2 cup (1 stick) margarine
1 (12-ounce) can evaporated milk
1 (16-ounce) package marshmallows
2 cups chocolate morsels
2 1/2 cups chopped pecans
1 teaspoon vanilla extract

Mix sugar, margarine, and milk. Cook for 7-12 minutes after mixture starts to boil. Add remaining ingredients. Pour into greased pan, cool, and cut into squares.

Chocolate Candy Balls

2 (1-pound) boxes powdered sugar, sifted
1 (14-ounce) can sweetened condensed milk
1/4 cup (1 stick) margarine, melted
1 teaspoon vanilla extract
1 quart chopped pecans
1/4 pound household paraffin
1/2 pound (2 sticks) margarine
2-3 teaspoons unsweetened cocoa powder

Mix together and form into balls. Cool. Melt
paraffin; add margarine and cocoa. Dip candy
balls into this latter mixture to have a chocolate
coating.

Buttermilk Candy

1 teaspoon soda
1 cup buttermilk
3 cups sugar
2 tablespoons corn syrup
1 cup chopped pecans
1 teaspoon vanilla extract
2 tablespoons margarine

Dissolve soda in buttermilk. Add syrup and
sugar. Mix well and cook until soft ball stage
forms. Add vanilla, margarine, and pecans.
Pour into greased pan.

Gum Drop Cookies

2 cups all-purpose flour
1/4 teaspoon salt
1 teaspoon ground cinnamon
1 cup gum drops
1/2 cup chopped pecans
4 eggs
1 tablespoon cold water
2 cups brown sugar

Sift flour, salt, and cinnamon. Cut gum drops with kitchen shears and dredge with pecans in a small portion of the flour. Beat eggs and water, add sugar and remaining flour; blend well. Add pecans and gum drops. Spread in greased and floured pan. Bake at 325 degrees about 30 minutes. Frost with icing.

Icing:
3 tablespoons margarine
2 tablespoons orange juice
1 teaspoon grated orange rind
3/4 cup powdered sugar

While gum drop cookies are warm, make this icing and spread on cookies. Melt margarine. Add orange rind and juice. Stir in sugar and spread mixture onto cookies. Cool. Cut into squares.

Yvonne has given a whole new meaning to brownies "from scratch". The recipe on the next page for her Brownies is easy and so much better than any mix that comes in a box.

Brownies

1 cup (2 sticks) margarine
3 (1-ounce) squares unsweetened chocolate
2 cups sugar
4 eggs
1 cup all-purpose flour
1 teaspoon vanilla extract
1 cup chopped pecans

Bake at 325 degrees for about 30 minutes in a
13-by-9-by-2-inch pan. Cool slightly and
spread with your favorite chocolate icing.

This recipe from Eleene seems almost too simple to be true
for such yummy results.

Graham Cracker Pralines

12 whole graham crackers
1 cup light brown sugar
1 cup (2 sticks) margarine
1 cup chopped pecans

Combine sugar, margarine, and pecans and
boil for 2 minutes. Place crackers on a cookie
sheet and pour mixture onto crackers. Bake at
300 degrees for 15 minutes. Cool for 10 minutes. Then cut.

Mable got the recipe for these wonderful Toffee Nut Bars from a 1938 PTA cookbook and baked them every Christmas that I can remember. Now they're part of my annual Christmas cookie-baking repertoire and have been served at many of our Christmas open houses.

Toffee Nut Bars

1 cup (2 sticks) margarine
1 cup brown sugar
1 egg yolk
1 teaspoon vanilla extract
2 cups all-purpose flour
2 teaspoons ground cinnamon
1 egg white
1 cup chopped pecans

Sift flour and cinnamon. Set aside. Cream margarine and brown sugar, then add egg yolk and vanilla. Add flour mixture gradually. Pat to 1/4-inch thick on a greased sheet or rectangular pan. Spread top with 1 unbeaten egg white. Sprinkle with pecans. Bake at 300 degrees for 30 minutes. Cut into bars.

The Oatmeal Scotchies on the next page are a special favorite of Matthew's. They went with him to school, on choir trips, to youth camps, and were served at his high-school graduation party. They are a nice diversion from the old standby Chocolate Chip cookies.

Oatmeal Scotchies

1 cup all-purpose flour
1 teaspoon baking soda
1/2 teaspoon each salt and ground cinnamon
1 cup (2 sticks) margarine, softened
3/4 cup sugar
3/4 cup firmly packed brown sugar
2 eggs
1 teaspoon vanilla extract
3 cups oats, uncooked
1 12-ounce package butterscotch chips

In a small bowl, combine flour, soda, salt, and cinnamon. Set aside. In a large bowl, combine margarine, sugar, brown sugar, eggs, and vanilla. Beat until light and fluffy. Gradually add flour mixture. Stir in oats and chips. Drop by tablespoonfuls onto ungreased sheets. Bake at 375 degrees for 7-8 minutes. Makes 4 dozen.

This is another favorite from Bonnie's candy recipe collection.

Date Nut Candy

2 cups sugar
2 tablespoons Karo® syrup
1 cup water or milk
1 cup nuts

Cook sugar, syrup, and water or milk until miture forms a soft ball. Add nuts. Form into one long roll and roll in damp cloth Slice when mixture cools.

Mable baked these Lemon Bars and served them on the historic day when she and my dad met my birthmother and her husband for the first time. On that day, my family of genetic origin came together with my adoptive family and shared years of recollections as they dined on these delightful, lemony treats. For us, this recipe is truly worth saving!

Lemon Bars

1 cup (2 sticks) margarine
2 cups all-purpose flour
1/2 cup powdered sugar
4 eggs
6 tablespoons fresh lemon juice
2 cups sugar
4 tablespoons all-purpose flour
1 teaspoon baking powder
1/2 teaspoon salt

Preheat oven to 350 degrees. Put margarine in 13-by-9-by-2-inch pan; insert into oven and melt. Mix 2 cups flour and powdered sugar. Stir this mixture into the melted margarine in the 13-by-9-by-2-inch pan and press down into pan until it forms a crust. Bake at 350 degrees for 20 minutes. Mix eggs, lemon juice, sugar, 4 tablespoons flour, baking powder, and salt. Bake at 350 degrees for 25 minutes. Sift powdered sugar over top. Cool and cut into squares.

The recipe that follows for Brown Betty was a favorite of the Red-Haired Miller Girls as they grew up. Mattie made it for them, and then Bonnie carried on the tradition, baking it for her family. It's a quick way to use apples you may have on hand and to dash out a quick mealtime dessert. It's especially good to serve with ice cream or whipped topping.

Brown Betty

2 1/2 cups apples, peeled and diced
1 cup bread crumbs
1/2 cup sugar
1/2 teaspoon ground cinnamon
2 tablespoons margarine
1/3 cup water

Peel and dice apples and set them aside. Mix bread crumbs, sugar, and cinnamon. Cut in margarine with pastry cutter. Spray 7x11 glass pan with cooking spray. Layer half of crumb mixture on the bottom of pan. Layer all apples next. Finish with rest of crumbs. Pour water over all. Bake at 350 degrees for 30-35 minutes, or until apples are tender. Serves 6-8.

Everything that Mattie cooked seemed like magic, but this Magic Pie is indeed a memorable dessert, especially on a hot summer day.

Magic Pie

1 (3-ounce) package lemon-flavored gelatin
3/4 cup hot water
scant cup sugar
juice of 2 lemons (plus grated rind of 1 lemon)
1 (14-ounce) can sweetened condensed milk,
    whipped
vanilla wafers

Combine dissolved gelatin, sugar, lemon juice, lemon rind, and whipped condensed milk. Mix thoroughly. Thoroughly line the bottom of a pie plate with whole vanilla wafers. Serves 6-8.

Another of Mattie's dishes that has summertime written all over it is her Pineapple Ice Box Cake. It's like eating a pineapple-flavored cloud.

Pineapple Ice-Box Cake

1 cup water
1 cup sugar
1 envelope unflavored gelatin
1/2 cup water
1 (10-ounce) package miniature marshmallows
1 (20-ounce) can crushed pineapple
1 ready-made angel food cake
juice of 2 oranges
1/2 pint whipping cream
1/3 cup sugar
1/2 teaspoon almond extract

Boil 1 cup water and 1 cup sugar. Set aside. In another bowl, soak gelatin in 1/2 cup water. Pour sugar/water mixture into gelatin/water mixture. Allow to cool. Combine undrained pineapple and juice of two oranges. Add to gelatin mixture. Pour marshmallows into a bowl. Pour gelatin/fruit juice/sugar-water mixture over marshmallows. In 7x11 pan, alternate layers of cut-up angel food cake with layers of marshmallow mixture. Cover with whipped cream seasoned with sugar and almond extract. Chill in refrigerator for two hours before serving.

Bill and Jana's beautiful Shelley named this recipe for Chocolate Marshmallow Bars as her favorite one to prepare.

Chocolate-Marshmallow Bars

3/4 cup (1 1/2 sticks) margarine
1 1/2 cups sugar
3 eggs
1 teaspoon vanilla extract
1 1/3 cups flour
1/2 teaspoon baking powder
1/2 teaspoon salt
3 tablespoons unsweetened cocoa powder
1/2 cup chopped pecans (optional)
4 cups miniature marshmallows

Topping:
1 1/3 cups (8 ounces) chocolate morsels
3 tablespoons margarine
1 cup peanut butter
2 cups rice cereal

In a mixing bowl, cream margarine and sugar. Add eggs and vanilla; beat until fluffy. Combine flour, baking powder, salt, and cocoa; add to creamed mixture. Stir in pecans, if desired. Spread in a greased jelly roll pan. Bake at 350 degrees for 15-18 minutes. Sprinkle marshmallows evenly over cake; return to oven for 2-3 minutes. Using a knife dipped in water, spread the melted marshmallows evenly over cake. Cool. For topping, combine in a small saucepan chocolate morsels, margarine, and peanut butter. Cook over low heat, stirring constantly, until melted and well blended. Remove from heat; stir in cereal. Spread over bars. Chill. Makes about 3 dozen bars.

This cookbook appropriately concludes with a recipe for Old-Fashioned Custard, because the story behind it represents the essence of what *Way Back in the Country* is all about. Eleene says this recipe is the first one Yvonne, her mother-in-law, shared with her after Eleene joined the family by marriage.

Recipes passed down through the generations tell a family's story. Please write down your own treasured tales so they won't be lost in time!

Old-Fashioned Custard

    1 1/2 cups sugar
    2 heaping tablespoons all-purpose flour
    2 eggs
    1 1/4 cups milk
    1 teaspoon vanilla extract

Mix sugar and flour. Add two egg yolks (reserve whites) and milk until mixture is thin. Cook until thick, stirring constantly. Beat egg whites and fold into mixture. Add vanilla. Refrigerate. If you like, you may serve this with a dollop of whipped topping on top.

Index

To order more copies of
Way Back in the Country

Contact:
Hannibal Books
P.O. Box 461592
Garland, Texas 75046

Fax: 1-972-487-7960
Phone: 1-800-747-0738
Email: hannibalbooks@earthlink.net
Visit: www.hannibalbooks.com

Or use order form on page 183 of this book.

Order other books from Hannibal Books

Way Back in the Country by Kay Moore. Join the antics of the Three Red-Haired Miller Girls as their farm family shares six generations of recipes and the stories behind them.

_____ **Copies at $9.95 =** _____

When the Heart Soars Free by Kay Moore. A heart-touching love story with a healing, biblical message. Set in a picturesque mountain wonderland.

_____ **Copies at $9.95 =** _____

Gathering the Missing Pieces in an Adopted Life by Kay Moore. Pulitzer-Prize nominee seeks her birth-family roots; includes helps from numerous others impacted by adoption.

_____ **Copies at $9.95 =** _____

Way Back When by James C. Hefley. Ozark Mountain history comes to life in this fully documented narrative. The author's personal story to learn more about his family roots helps all readers appreciate their ties to the long ago.

_____ **Copies at $7.95 =** _____

Way Back in the Hills (Book 2) by James C. Hefley. James Carl Hefley, 13, child prodigy of Big Creek Valley, enrolls at Arkansas Tech as one of its youngest students ever. Many eye-opening experiences await this country boy.

_____ **Copies at $7.95 =** _____

Please add $3.00 postage and handling for first book, plus 50-cents for each additional book.

Shipping & handling _____
TX residents add sales tax _____
TOTAL ENCLOSED_____
check _____ or Credit card #_____ exp. date_____
(Visa, MasterCard, Discover, American Express accepted)

Name_____

Address_____

City _____ State _____ Zip _____

MAIL TO: HANNIBAL BOOKS
P.O. BOX 461592
Garland, TX 75046-1592
OR CALL: 1-800-747-0738
or order from www.hannibalbooks.com